EPHESUS

SELAHATTİN ERDEMGİL

Archaeologist, Director of the Ephesus Museum

NET

TURİSTİK YAYINLAR
SANAYİ VE TİCARET A.Ş.

Cover: Head of Eros.
Back cover: The Celsus Library.

Published and distributed by :

NET TURİSTİK YAYINLAR A.Ş.

Yerebatan Caddesi, 15/3, 34410 Cağaloğlu, Istanbul-Turkey
Tel.: (90-1) 520 84 06 - 527 42 70 Fax: (90-1) 513 64 31

1363. Sokak, 1, Kat: 5, 35230 Çankaya, İzmir-Turkey
Tel.: (90-51) 12 30 01 - 25 38 61 Fax: (90-51) 19 75 71

Sedir Mahallesi, Gazi Bulvarı, Akdemir Apt., Kat 1, D.6-7 Antalya-Turkey
Tel.: (90-31) 16 99 94 Fax: (90-31) 16 99 93

Yenimahalle, Nev-Yap Sitesi, 5. Blok, D.1, Nevşehir-Turkey
Tel.: (90-4851) 3089-4620 Fax: (90-4851) 40 36

Text: **Selahattin Erdemgil,** Archaologist, Director of the Ephesus Museum
Translation: **Nükhet Eraslan**
Photographs: **Nusret Nurdan Eren,**
T. Birgili (29, 30, 31, 40, 41), **C. Tütüncü** (63, 106, 119, 123), **M. Büyükkolancı** (15, 25, 99),
Y. Canbaş (138, 139), **M. A. Döğenci** (12), **C. Koççoban** (34, 35)
Layout: **Not Ajans**
Typsetting: **AS Dizgi**
Colour separation: **Çali Grafik A.Ş.**
Printed in Turkey by: **Asır Matbaacılık Ltd. Şti.**

ISBN 975-479-080-9

Copyright ©1986 NET TURİSTİK YAYINLAR A.Ş.
All rights reserved.
3ᵗʰ Edition, 1990

CONTENTS

Its Name and Establishment	6	The Brothel	82
The Lydian Period	10	The Monumental Gate	
The Persian Period	12	(the Gate of Hadrian)	83
The Age of Alexander the Great	15	The Celsus Library	84
The Roman Period	18	The Mazeus-Mithridates Gate and	
St. Paul and St. John	19	the Commercial Agora	86
The Meeting of the Third		The Temple of Scrapis	89
Ecumenical Council	21	The Marble Road	93
The Excavations	25	The Theatre	93
The Temple of Artemis	26	The Hellenistic Fountain	98
The City Walls and		The Harbour Street	98
the Magnesia Gate	32	The Theatre Gymnasium	99
The Varius Baths	36	The Verulanus Sports Arena	100
The Aqueducts and		The Harbour Gymnasium	
the Nympheum (the Fountain)		and Its Palaestra	100
The State Agora	38	The Harbour Baths	101
The Basilica	39	The Harbour	101
The Odeion	41	The Church of the Virgin Mary	
The Imperial Cult and Temples	45	(the Council Church)	102
Official Establishments of		The Byzantine Baths	104
the City and the Prytaneion	49	The Acropolis	104
The Memmius Monument	53	The Fountain	104
The Fountain	54	The Stadium	105
The Pollio Fountain	55	The Vedius Gymnasium	106
The Temple of Domitian	57	The Cave of the Seven Sleepers	106
The Inscription Gallery	60	The Church of St. John	107
The G. Laecanius Bassus Fountain	62	The Hall of the Residential Relics of	
The Curetes Street	64	the Museum of Ephesus	122
The Trajan Fountain	65	The Hall of the Fountain Relics	132
The Round Tower	68	The Hall of the Recent Finds	135
The Scholastikia Baths	68	The Courtyard	140
The Temple of Hadrian	72	The Baths	145
Houses on the slopes	74	The Hall of the Funerary Relics	145
Peristyle House I	76	The Hall of Artemis	149
Peristyle House II	78	The Hall of Imperial Cults	
The Octagon	81	and Portraits	154
The Byzantine Fountain	82	Bibliography	158

ITS NAME AND ESTABLISHMENT

One day early in the summer of 54 A.D. thousands of Ephesians crowded the great theatre, roused by the silver-smith Demetrius. St. Paul's new teaching that gods made with hands are not gods at all, was threatening the lucrative trade in silver shrines of Artemis Ephesia. For two hours they kept shouting "Great is Artemis of the Ephesians". St. Paul, dressed in white and holding a sceptre in one hand, failed to calm the wild crowd. With the help of a few of his followers he eventually escaped, barely saving his own life. This day was one of the most important days in the history of Ephesus, like the day its founder Androklos came to the city, the times when first the Lydians and later the Persians invaded the city, the days earthquakes struck in the years 17,355,365 and 368 A.D., and the day the Ecumenical Council met in 431. Actually, the screams of "Great is Artemis of the Ephesians" were the dying breath of the seven thousand year old mother goddess.

The mother goddess whom we know as Artemis Ephesia, acquired her form as an extremely fertile woman, in 7000 B.C., at the hands of the Çatalhöyük people and started her long reign. She was the mother of everything, she was the most powerful being and she ruled everything. Her influence spread to the four corners of Anatolia, then to Mesopotamia, Egypt, Arabia and even to Scandinavia. The mother goddess, after thousands of years of evolution became Artemis Ephesia. The Temple of Artemis built

See page 157 for key.

in her honour, was known as the most famous treasure of the past, and Ephesus located in its vicinity, was considered the cradle of civilization from the cultural and social points of view.

Our sources of information on Ephesus are works of ancient writers thousands of inscriptions unearthed during the excavations, and other archaeological finds. Yet our information on the establishment of Ephesus is insufficient. Strabo and Pausanias, famous writers of antiquity, indicate that Ephesus was founded by the Amazons, and the majority of the population of Ephesus consisted of Carians and Lelegians.

According to the historian Herodotus, the Carians considered themselves the oldest inhabitants of Anatolia. They lived in the area called Caria, and Halicarnassus was its most important city. Whereas the Lelegians migrated from Thrace and the Aegean islands into Asia Minor, Amazons occupy an important place in the legends related to the establishment of the city. This may be why Strabo mentions that Ephesus was named after an Amazon.

The Ephesian poet Kallinos who lived during the end of the 7th century and the beginning of the 6th century B.C., wrote that the Amazon who captured Ephesus was named Smyrna (İzmir). According to the poet Hipponax who was from Ephesus, but in 540 B.C. was expelled from the city by Athenagoras, a section of Ephesus was called Smyrna.

Strabo indicates that Smyrna was located between Lepre Akte and Thrakeia and that Lepre Akte was Mt. Pion (Bülbül Dağı) and Thrakeia was Mt. Koressos (Panayır Dağı). Later Smyrnaians left Ephesus and resettled near today's İzmir and established the city of İzmir. The interest of

2- Mycenean bowls. 14th - 13th century B.C.

Ephesus in the Amazons lasted throughout history. That is why in the 5th century B.C., a competition called the Amazon Statue Competition was held among the leading sculptors of the age, to choose the statue to be placed at the Temple of Artemis (see Temple of Artemis). The relics from a Mycenaean grave excavated near the Church of St. John and exhibited at the Ephesus Museum, are the earliest examples of archaeological finds discovered so far in Ephesus. These have been dated to 1400-1300 B.C.. Based on this information we must accept that Ephesus was established about this time. The bowls unearthed, used to be marketed in the colonies Mycenaeans established along the shores of the Mediterranean and Western Anatolia, and they display the most advanced techniques of the day. These bowls were found along the shore stretching from Troy to Halicarnassus. Those found in Miletus near Ephesus have been dated to 1600 B.C. and they are considered the oldest. Professor Akurgal and other archaeologists suggest that the late Kingdom of Ahhiyava which is mentioned in the 13th and 14th century B.C. Hittite sources, was located near the region of Miletus. If this is proven, then, due to its location, Ephesus must have been an important city in the kingdom, in other words, it must have been the city called Apasas in the Hittite tablets. But so far, no Mycenaean settlement in Ephesus has been discovered.

The years between 1300-1100 B.C. were a period of instability in Anatolia, Syria and Egypt. Hittites who ruled in Central Anatolia were fac-

3- Detail of the frieze of Temple of Hadrian. Androklos and the Boar. Marble. 2nd century A.D.

ed with uprisings in the states under their rule.

After the fall of Troy and ensuing looting, the Thracians started migrating south. They joined the other Thracian groups who came from the sea and settled in Western Anatolia, forming colonies. The written Egyptian sources of the 12th century, mention the destruction of cities during these migrations with deep sorrow. During the time of these migrations, regions called Aeolis and Ionia appeared on the map. The region of Ionia where Ephesus is located is referred to as "Yavan" in the Bible, "Yavnai" in the Assyrian inscriptions and as "Yauna" in the Persian inscriptions. To ensure their security, the immigrants preferred to settle on islands near the coast and on peninsulas. The colonization of Ephesus, as in the other Ionian cities, was completed in the 10th century B.C. Strabo and Pausanias tell the story of the settlement: Androklos, son of Kodros (the King of Athens), and his friends who were about to migrate to Anatolia, could not decide on the location of the new city they were going to establish. They consulted the oracle of Apollo, which told them to establish their new city at the location which would be indicated by a fish and a boar. Androklos and his friends who came to the region wanted to cook fish, but the fish they were frying jumped off the pan, scattering flames that set the dry bushes on fire. A boar ran out of the burning bushes and Androklos started to chase the boar, caught it and killed it. Convinced that the prophesy of the oracle had come true, Androklos and his friends established their new city in this location at the northern foot of Mt. Pion which was like an inner harbour

4- The Celsus Library. Early 2nd century A.D

then. To commemorate the occasion, they built the Temple of Athena on the spot where the boar had been killed. The exact location of that temple is still unknown.

Kondros, the King of Athens and father of Androklos, was famous for his courage. Before a war with his neighbours, he consulted the Delphi oracle, which told him "The armies of the king who dies first will be the victors". During the fighting, King Kodros had himself killed intentionally by the enemy. The ensuing fight for the throne of Athens between Androklos and his stepbrothers who were kings in the cities near Athens, triggered his emigration to Anatolia.

Ephesus existed here for 400 years and was ruled by Androklos and his descendents. When Androklos died during a war with the Carians he was buried near the Magnesia Gate and a heroon (a shrine dedicated to a deified person) was built on the site.

THE LYDIAN PERIOD

In the 7th century B.C., Ephesus and the other Ionian cities were attacked by the Cimmerians. It is not known for sure whether the Cimmerians captured Ephesus or not. The relics discovered during excavations indicate that the Temple of Artemis was burnt and demolished. Only a few typically Cimmerian objects have been discovered in Ephesus. The ivory figure of a ram displayed in the Hall of Artemis is one of these Cimmerian treasures.

Ephesus recovered and rapidly regained its power after the Cimmerian devastation.

The 6th century B.C. was one of the most glorious periods in the history of Ephesus. The minstrel Kallinos, Hipponax, and the famous philosopher Heraclitus lived during this period. Heraclitus especially, who accepted fire as the basic element and suggested that everything evolved, acquired great fame in the Ionian school. Heraclitus dedicated his work called "Nature", a section of which is still extant, to the Temple of Artemis.

The fame of Ephesus spread everywhere at that time, and this is why King Croesus of Lydia attacked Ephesus first (560 B.C.). During the attack, Ephesians stretched a rope from the Temple of Artemis to the city, and retreated behind the rope believing that the goddess would save them. Unfortunately, their expectations did not come true and the Lydian army entered the city.

Contrary to what was expected, Croesus treated the Ephesians as friends, yet, he forced them to leave the city in Koressos and establish another city in the vicinity of the Temple of Artemis. Since this second settlement has been covered by soil deposited by the river Kaystros (Küçük Menderes), today, it is buried 10 metres under the ground. Therefore it is impossible to excavate beyond the area around the Temple of Artemis.

When the Lydians captured Ephesus, the archaic Temple of Artemis (564-546 B.C.) was still under construction. To please the goddess and the Ephesians, Croesus presented column capitals with reliefs, and gold statues of calves to the temple. One of the column capitals had his name

5- The Artemision.

inscribed on it. (All these column capitals and many of the objects discovered in the temple in the course of excavations which started in 1869, were taken to the British Museum). During this period, a fortification wall which started at the harbour was built around the city. The Artemision and its vicinity was also included in the area surrounded by this fortification wall.

THE PERSIAN PERIOD

In the middle of the 6th century B.C., Anatolia was faced with the attacks of the Persians from the east. Before attacking Western Anatolia, the Persians sent ambassadors to the cities in Aeolis and Ionia to persuade them to join in a revolt against Croesus, but they failed. Following the defeat of Croesus by the Persian King Cyrus, Aeolis and Ionia declared their acceptance of Persian rule instead of Lydian rule, under the same conditions.

According to Herodotus, King Cyrus responded by telling them the following story:

One day, a flautist started playing his flute in order to attract fish to the shore, but he was ignored. Then, he found a fisherman's net and caught a lot of fish. He looked at the fish jumping in the net and said, 'While I was playing the flute, none of you came to the shore and danced, so don't dance now either'.

Upon hearing the response of King Cyrus, all the twelve cities in Ionia, except Miletus, retreated to their states and started preparing to defend themselves. They also asked for help from Sparta. The Milesians did not feel the need to prepare themselves, because they had already signed a treaty with the Persians. The help requested from Sparta never arrived, and in 547 B.C., Harpagos, one of the famous commanders of Cyrus, starting with Phokaia, captured the whole of Western Anatolia. Thus, Ephesus for the second time in its history, came under the rule of another foreign state.

The Persians, as they did with every state they ruled, let the Ephesians rule themselves and practise their own religion. They did not harm the Temple of Artemis either. Ephesus maintained its economic power and continued its trade and cultural relations. The Persians united Caria, Lycia, Pamphylia and Ionia to form the Ionian Satrapy and began to rule the area under a satrap. During the Persian rule, Ephesus prospered and became an important centre for arts and culture.

Persians forced Ephesus and the other cities to pay tribute and provided ships and soldiers when needed. This attitude of the Persians created such friction that the people of the Ionian cities almost wished for a tyrant.

After Cyrus, during the reigns of Cambyses and Darius, the tribute they had to pay was increased so much, that finally the Ionian cities united and started the historic "Ionian Revolt" in 500 B.C.. Aristogoras, the tyrant of Miletus, led the revolt in which Ephesus played a key role. The rebels first came to Ephesus and under the guidance of the Ephesians, by following the banks of Kaystros, they reached Sardes (the capital of the Persian Satrapy) in three days. They captured the capital without a fight and

6- Artemis Ephesia.
Marble. 1st century
A.D..

destroyed the city till there was not even a house left. The destruction of the Temple of Cybele during the revolt, was used as an excuse later when the Persians destroyed the temples in Greece. The Ionian Revolt came to an end when in 494 B.C. the Ionian fleet was defeated by the Persians near the island of Lade near Miletus.

Immediately following their victory, the Persians recaptured the whole of Ionia and looted and destroyed many cities. Miletus and Chios (Sakız) suffered the heaviest losses. Many ships from Chios were sunk and they were chased by the Persians. They took refuge along the shores of Mykale, west of Priene. After pulling their ships on to land, they walked through the night and came to Ephesus where the Thesmophoria Festival was being celebrated. Only the married women used to attend the Thesmophoria Festival celebrations which took place in October and November. The Ephesians mistook the armed Chians they saw at night, as bandits who had come to kidnap their women and killed every one of them.

In 479 B.C., the Persian commander Mardonios recaptured Athens and central Greece, but at Plataia, he was defeated by the allied armies and killed. Shortly after his defeat, his armies were forced to retreat. The Spartans attacked the Persian fleet which was on land at Mykale and burned it. Following the victory over the Persians in Plataia and Mykale, the Ionian cities rebelled. In order to eliminate the Persians from Anatolia as well as from Greece, in 478 B.C., under the leadership of Sparta and Athens, the "Attic-Delos Naval Association" was formed. According to Thukydides and Aristotle, Ephesus paid 7.5 talents in 453 B.C., 6 talents in 444 B.C., and 7.5 talents in 436 B.C. to the association. According to the rules established by the Athenian statesman Aristeides, the payments were adjusted in proportion to the wealth of the city. Therefore, the dues paid by

7- The Artemision.
F. Adler (1873).

Ephesus indicate that it was one of the richest cities.

During the Peloponnesian Wars in the last quarter of the 5th century, Ephesus sided first with Athens, then with Sparta. Following the collaboration between the Spartans and the Persians in the summer of 409 B.C., Athenian Thrasyllos came to Samos from Athens with 50 ships that were fully equipped for land warfare. After a three day stay in Samos they attacked Pygela near Kuşadası and started to raid the city. The Milesians unsuccessfully attacked a few times but finally they were defeated.

Next day, the Athenians went to Notion, located about 10 km. north of Ephesus. Notion was under their rule. From there, they attacked nearby Kolophon and Metropolis (Torbalı) the same night and raided the villages, burning the crops. The Persian commander Stages who was in charge of defence of the area, attacked the Athenians but could not stop them from escaping to Notion.

The Ionian satrap Tissaphernes suspected that Thrasyllos would attack Ephesus, and he invited soldiers from each city to defend the sacred city of Artemis. During the battle known as the Battle of Ephesus, the Athenians suffered heavy losses and under the truce they collected their dead soldiers and retreated to Notion once again.

After burying their dead there, they set sail for the Dardanelles. While resting at Mytilene, they saw twenty-five Syracuson merchant ships on their way to the Dardanelles from Ephesus and attacked them. They captured four ships and chased the others to Ephesus but could not catch them. In the spring of 407 B.C., the Spartans appointed a very able soldier named Lysander, as the commander of the forces in Anatolia. After consulting, Cyrus who had come to Sardes, Lysander, with the help of Cyrus, increased the number of ships in his fleet to ninenty. A strong Athenian fleet which was at Samos then under the command of Alkibiades, pulled in near the coast of Notion in order to be closer to the Spartan fleet in the Ephesus harbour. Upon hearing that another Athenian fleet had seized Phokaia, Alkibiades went to help with a squadron of ships. He left one of his assistants, Antiokhos in charge, and told him not to go to war to during his absence, but Antiokhos attacked two enemy ships on a reconnaissance mission, and when help arrived from both sides, a battle started off the coast of Notion. At the end of the battle, the Athenians had lost some of their ships and retreated to Samos. Alkibiades later attacked Ephesus but could not get any results.

THE AGE OF ALEXANDER THE GREAT

After achieving unity in Macedonia and Greece, Alexander concentrated on eliminating the Persians from Anatolia. When he crossed the Dardanelles, the Persian's Ionian satrap Spithridates, in order to stop Alexander, joined the Persian army stationed near the Granikos stream (Rize Çayı). Arrian, one of the famous writers of antiquity, called this war the Battle of the Cavalry. During the fighting, Spithridates, who was about to strike Alexander with his sword, was killed by a Macedonian.

Alexander the Great defeated the Persians, entered Sardes, and transfer-

red the rule of all the areas under the satrapy of Spithridates to Asandros, son of Philotas. He stayed in Sardes for a while and then went to Ephesus after a four day journey.

When the Greek mercenaries heard the news of the defeat of the Persians and the death of the satrap, they captured two Persian warships anchored in Ephesus harbour and escaped. This is why in 334 B.C., Alexander entered Ephesus without encountering any resistance. First, he brought back those who were forced out of the city because of him, and announced an end to the oligarchy by declaring the establishment of a people's democracy. He also ordered that the tribute and duties which were being paid to the Persians, instead be given to the Temple of Artemis. He sacrificed animals at the temple, organised his army and ordered a procession.

The architect Kheirocrates (according to Vitruvius, the architect Deinocrates), was restoring the Temple of Artemis which had been burnt the night Alexander was born, by a mentally unstable man named Herostratos, who wanted his name etched in history. According to what Strabo wrote based on Artemidoros, Alexander announced to the Ephesians that he wanted to pay for all the previous and the subsequent expenses for the restoration of the Temple of Artemis. Yet, upon hearing an Ephesian, whose name we do not know and whom Artemidoros praised highly, say, "It is not appropriate for a god to present gifts to another god", Alexander changed his mind. Since he was very pleased with the work of the architect, he entrusted the establishment of the city of Alexandria on the Nile delta to the same architect after he completed his work at the Temple of Artemis. Following the death of Alexander, Ephesus lived through dark days. After changing hands a few times among the generals, finally in 287 B.C. it began to be ruled by Lysimachos.

In 299 B.C., Lysimachos married Arsinoe, daughter of the Egyptian king Ptolemaios I, his old friend, for selfish reasons. He rebuilt the city located between Mt. Pion and Mt. Koressos and surrounded it by a fortification wall. Lysimachos also renamed the city Arsinoe but the name did not gain acceptance. When the people living in the vicinity of the Artemision refused to settle in this new city, the canals of the city were stopped up to cause flooding and thus, the Ephesians were forced to migrate.

Arsinoe, who was an ambitious woman, feared that Agathocles, Lysimachos' son by his first wife, would become the king instead of her son. So, she convinced Lysimachos that his first son was planning to kill him. Consequently, Lysimachos had his son Agathocles killed. Fearing for their lives, Agathocles' widow and a few commanders, sought the protection of Seleukos and provoked him against Lysimachos. Seleukos, taking advantage of the recent developments, attacked the land of Lysimachos and the two armies clashed in the Korou Pedion plain, east of Manisa. Lysimachos who was an old man, died during the fight and his land was captured by Seleukos (281 B.C.).

Antiochos II, one of the Seleucid kings fought the Ptolemies in Egypt for years. The Egyptian king Ptolemy Philadelphos told Antiochos II that, if he divorced his wife Laodike and married his daughter Benerike, he would present him with valuable gifts and sign a peace treaty with him. Antiochos II accepted his offer. He divorced his wife and exiled her to Ephesus. Thus, peace was achieved. Yet, after the death of Ptolemy Philadelphos in 246 B.C., Antiochos II followed his wife to Ephesus. He stayed in Ephesus for a while, but one day he was poisoned by his wife Laodike and died. His son Seleukos II succeeded him. It is thought that Antiochos II was buried

8- The Commercial Agora. Granite columns 1st century B.C.

in the Belevi Mausoleum.

Ephesus, during the time of Antiochos Theos, came under the rule of the Ptolemies in Egypt. In 196 B.C. during the rule of Antiochos III, the Seleucids recaptured Ephesus, and later, in 188 B.C. as a result of the Apemaia Peace Treaty, they lost it to the Pergamese Kingdom. In 133 B.C. when the Pergamese Kingdom was bequeathed to Rome, Ephesus came under the rule of Rome.

THE ROMAN PERIOD

Due to the heavy taxes enforced under the Roman Asian province system established in 129 B.C. and the unfavourable ruling policies, Ephesus joined the other cities in Western Anatolia and revolted in 880 B.C. siding with Mithridates VI, the King of Pontus. When Mithridates came to Ephesus, he ordered every Roman citizen living in the Asian province to be killed. Subsequently, eighty thousand people were massacred in one day. The monuments and the statues of Roman statesmen in Ephesus were also destroyed.

Shortly after the rebellion, Sulla, the commander of the Roman armies came to the Asian province, punished the rebels and again placed Ephesus under the rule of Rome. Famous Cicero, during his campaign against the Parthians in Eastern Anatolia, came to Ephesus on July 22nd 51 B.C. as the Cilician procouncil of Rome and planned his campaign here. When Antonius came to Ephesus from Central Anatolia following the War of Philoppoi, the Ephesians, knowing his predilection for Dionysiac festivals, dressed their women as Maenads and their men as satyrs and organized a welcoming ceremony.

Antonius sent his army to Cilicia during a period when his relations with Octavius were tense, and in 33 B.C. returned to Ephesus with Cleopatra. With the two hundred ships Cleopatra gave him, he increased the number of the ships in his fleet to eight hundred. Antonius, who was defeated by Octavius in a battle in Actium, escaped to Egypt in 31 B.C.. In the spring of the following year, Octavius came to Egypt by crossing Syria and seized Alexandria. Antonius and Cleopatra, in despair, committed suicide. Following the death of Antonius, in 27 B.C., Octavius became Emperor by the decision of the Senate and was renamed Augustus.

The most important change in Ephesus was brought about by Emperor Augustus. He declared Ephesus the capital of the province instead of Pergamum. Hence, Ephesus became the first and the largest metropolis in Asia, the most important trade centre, permanent residence of the governor of Rome, and one of the five largest cities in the Roman Empire. In 27 B.C. the Roman provinces were reorganized, and only those who had served as consuls were sent to Asia as governors. The Asian province together with the African province, became the largest province in the senate. The governorship of a province was one of the highest positions in the senate. In the beginning, the period between consulship and proconsulship was 5-10 years, but later it became 15 years. Since senators became consuls around the age of forty, the Asian governors who lived in Ephesus were not younger than 50 or 55, and since the governors served only a year, there were many people in Ephesus who had served as governors. Emperors Antonius Pius and Pupienus, had also served as governors in Ephesus.

In the summer of 123 A.D., Emperor Hadrian came to Ephesus on his way to Rhodes and took a trip to the islands in the Aegean on the yacht of a rich Ephesian. When he returned to Ephesus in 129 A.D., he restored the city, especially the harbour.

A Gothic fleet of five hundred ships left Crimea in 262 A.D. and went first to Kyzikos and then to Ephesus. They captured a section of the city and plundered it, including the Temple of Artemis. Following the brief Gothic attack, Ephesus tried to regain its power.

ST. PAUL AND ST. JOHN

During the 1st century A.D. in Ephesus, which was the largest and the most important city in antiquity, the Jews and others practised their own religion freely whether they believed in the Anatolian, Greek Roman or the Egyptian religions. Also, a new religion, Christianity, was just getting established in Jerusalem. The apostles who were trying to spread Christianity, were expelled from Jerusalem between 37-42 A.D. St. Paul came to Ephesus in 53. For three years, first in the synagogues and then everywhere in the city, he preached the gospel and gained followers. He also established the Church of Ephesus.

Christianity rapidly gained popularity in Ephesus. The jeweller Demetrius and others who earned a living by making and selling silver statues of Artemis, were quite distressed by the popularity of this new religion. Thousands of people provoked by Demetrius and his colleagues, met at the theatre of Ephesus and started shouting, "Great is Artemis Ephesia". They dragged St. Paul's friends Gaios and Aristarchos into the theatre amid the agitation. St. Paul wanted to face the crowd but those around him would not let him. Finally, the official in charge of the security of the city arrived and dispersed the crowd, and announced to those caught that the courts were open for those who had a complaint. Shortly after this event, St. Paul left Ephesus and went to Macedonia. Luke, the author of "Deeds of the Apostles" did not mention St. John when he wrote about the events which took place between 37-42. St. John was in Ephesus then with the Virgin Mary who had been entrusted to him. In 64, after St. Paul was decapitated outside the city wall of Rome, St. John became the leader of the Church in Ephesus.

In spite of his old age, St. John travelled the steppes of Anatolia and tried to spread Christianity. During the peak of antagonism toward Chris-

20

tianity in Pergamum and Izmir, St. John was taken to Rome tortured, and later was exiled to the island of Patmos where he wrote the 'Apocalypse'.

When the Roman emperor Domitian was stabbed to death by one of his servants, Christians were relieved. St. John returned to Ephesus and started writing his gospel. According to his will, he was buried in Ephesus. Today, his grave is in the church that bears his name.

9- A general view of the Church of St. John.

10- *A general view of the Church of St. John.*

THE MEETING OF THE THIRD ECUMENICAL COUNCIL

Since the Virgin Mary possessed many of the virtues of Artemis, the most magnificient goddess, the new religion gained popularity in Ephesus and spread quickly. Ephesus became important to Christians since St. Paul, St John and the Virgin Mary all lived here. The first church to be dedicated to her was constructed in Ephesus (see Mary-Council Church). The Third Ecumenical Council met in the Church of the Virgin Mary in 431. The principles of Christianity were established during this meeting.

Members of the council discussed the thesis that the Virgin Mary is not the mother of Jesus, the son of God, but the mother of Jesus, a mortal. Nestorius, the patriarch of Constantinople (İstanbul) first proposed this thesis when he was in Antiochia and later defended it vigorously in İstanbul. To prove his point, he claimed the authority of the Apostles for his views.

When the thesis created a turmoil, Emperor Theodosius himself attended the meeting of the Council in Ephesus. Nestorius, the patriarch of Constantinople; Cyril, the patriarch of Alexandria; John, the patriarch of Antiocheia; the representatives of Ephesus and the Pope were also present. Two hundred religious authorities discussed the issue. They also recorded for the

first time, in the proceedings of the meeting, that the Virgin Mary was buried in Ephesus.

In the 4th century, a basilica was built at the site of St. John's grave located on Ayasuluk hill (Ayasuluk Tepesi). Some Ephesians left Ephesus and settled around the basilica, since the harbour of Ephesus could no longer be used. When Emperor Justinian built the monumental church at the site of the basilica, almost all of the population of Ephesus moved into the vicinity of the Church of St. John.

In the 7th and 8th centuries, Ephesus, as well as the other cities in south-western Anatolia, was faced with the attacks of Arabs from the sea and looters from land. The fortress of Ayasuluk was reinforced against these attacks, and a fortification wall was constructed around the church which looked like an outer fortress. The armies of Caliph Suleiman spent the winter of 716 in Ephesus. During the 10th and 11th centuries, Ephesus was renamed Hagios Theologos in honour of St. John.

When Turks came to the area they found a small village, and Çaka Bey captured it easily from the Byzantines in 1304. Ibni Batuta who had visited Ayasuluk in the 14th century, mentioned that there were Venetian and Genoese consulates and a bishop in this large city.

During the rule of Aydınoğulları, Ephesus prospered again. Many mosques, large and small, and baths were constructed in the city and trade was revitalized. The famous İsa Bey Mosque was built in this period. Ephesus was completely deserted after the early Ottoman period.

11- The Church of the Virgin Mary. (the Council Church). 5th century A.D.

12- A general view of the Church of St. John.

*13- A general view of
the Church of St. John.*

*14- Apse of the Church
of St. John, 1988
Restoration project.*

THE EXCAVATIONS

The first archaeological excavations in Ephesus were started in 1869 by a British engineer J.T. Wood working for the British Museum. In 1863, Wood came to the area and unsuccessfully searched for the Temple of Artemis. An inscription found in the Theatre in 1869 mentioned that, the religious objects used in the plays were picked up from the temple, and following the sacred road, were brought into the city through the Magnesia Gate, and that these were taken back to the temple following the same route. Therefore, Wood had to find the Magnesia Gate first. Since Magnesia was an ancient city south-west of Ephesus, the Magnesia Gate had to be in that direction. By following the fortification walls of the Hellenistic period, Wood

15- The Church of St. John. Excavation of the sub-structure of the Atrium.

easily discovered the gate. Starting here, he carried on preliminary digs, and by following the road, he found the location of the temple. Yet, for various reasons he could not complete the excavation of the temple. After 1904, D.G. Hogarth resumed excavating the temple.

The excavations which are now being carried out by the Austrian Archaeological Institute, were started by Otto Benndorf in 1895. O. Benndorf obtained permission from the Ottoman sultan to excavate in Ephesus, and he later purchased a large section of the city. The land he had bought, was nationalized in recent years by the Turkish authorities. After Benndorf, under the supervision of (in chronological order) Profs. Keil, Miltner, Eichter, and since 1969 of Prof. Vetters, the main streets, squares, and the structures along the streets in Ephesus have been excavated. Prof. Vetters excavated a section of the insula with houses situated on the slopes and completed the restoration of two houses. The renovation of the Celsus Library was also realized in 1978 by Prof. Vetters. Most of the remains unearthed up to 1905 were taken to England, and most of those found between 1905 and 1923 were taken to Austria.

In 1954, the Ephesus Museum started excavating and restoring in Ephesus and since then, many important structures have been excavated and restored. The Ministry of Culture and Tourism of the Turkish Republic, in 1979, started the "Environmental Protection, Excavation and Restoration of Selçuk-Ephesus" project, with emphasis on the excavation of the Church of St. John, Stadium Street and the Church of the Virgin Mary.

1. THE TEMPLE OF ARTEMIS

The worship of Cybele-Artemis and the social structure of the temple:

Many statues of Cybele and Artemis have been discovered in Turkey. Those found in Çatalhöyük, (dated to 7000 B.C.) and Hacılar (dated to 6000 B.C.) are the oldest. These statuettes were made of baked clay, and since they were intended to look reproductive, their hips, breasts and genital organs were exaggerated. Although at first these were thought to be statues of Venus, later it was established that they represented the mother goddess. As time went by, the mother goddess changed form and her popularity spread everywhere in the prehistoric world. She acquired the local characteristics but never lost her essence. Although we do not know what the people of Çatalhöyük and Hacılar called the mother goddess, she was known as Isis in Egypt, Lat in Arab lands, Kubala, Cybele, Hepa and Artemis in Anatolia. Cybele was the most popular name in Anatolia and was worshipped the most. Her famous temple and cult centre is in Persinus Oren (village of Ballıhisar) of Sivrihisar near Ankara. The evolution of the mother goddess in antiquity reached a turning point in Pessinus which was an important centre in Phyrigia. Here, she seems diopetic (from the sky). In Pessinus, a meteorite similar in shape to her diopetic form was worshipped for many years as the statue of Cybele. In the reliefs found in many locations in Phyrigia (some of them on rocks), the figure of the mother goddess was carved without detail, similar to her diopetic form. During the reign of Attalos I, the King of Pergamum, the meteorite was taken to Rome, in the hope that it would help end the war between Rome and Carthage with the victory of Rome. It was erected on Platina hill.

The mother goddess also has a Xoanic form. Xoanic means "carved out of wood". The oldest statue of Artemis in Ephesus is thought to be of Xoanic type, carved out of wood without detail.

16- The Artemision.

The mother goddess who was taken to Rome from Pessinus, received a great deal of respect. Elagabalus, one of the Roman emperors, during a ceremony, cut off his male organ as required according to the worship of Cybele, and presented it to the mother goddess. The incident proves the respect she received in Rome.

The fact that Cybele-Artemis always looked definitely eastern becomes evident when her statues in the Ephesus Museum are examined. The legs of the statues are motionless as though fused. Although the nodes on her chest were once thought to be breasts, it has become apparent that they represent the testes of bulls sacrificed for her. Testes symbolize fertility since they produce "seeds". The bulls, lions and sphinxes that are on her skirt, indicate that she was the protectress of animals. The lions depicted on both sides of Cybele in her reliefs are seen on her arms in these statues.

The hierarchy among the priests in the temple was different from the hierarchy in the West. Even the terms used were different from the terms used by the Greeks, although during the Roman period, Greek was used. The temple was administered by only a few priests. The male organs of these priests and the head priest called Megaysos, were removed. According to Strabo, the priests were chosen from the middle of Anatolia and especially from the east. Becoming Megabysos meant assuming a very honourable duty. The assistants of Megabysos were virgins similar to the Vestal Virgins of Rome.

Some say that the worship of Artemis, the Temple of Artemis and the religious hierarchy were all modelled on the social structure of bees. The bee was the symbol of Ephesus, and it is often seen on coins and statues in Ephesus.

Another class of priests who served Artemis was called the Curetes. According to mythology, Curetes were demigods related to Zeus. While Zeus was creating Dionysus from his leg, Curetes stayed by him and made a noise so that Hera could not hear anything. Also, while Leto was giving birth to Artemis, Curetes stayed by her and made a noise. Every year this event was celebrated by a festival in Ortygia known as the birthplace of Artemis.

There was another class of twenty priests who were thought to be probably involved with the dances which took place during ceremonies. They may be referred to as "the acrobats" or "the tiptoers". The worship of Artemis and Cybele was the most important factor in the development of Ephesus. The number of priests, priestesses and guards reached hundreds.

The Temple of Artemis in Ephesus also served as a bank. The Megabysos was in charge of accepting gifts either presented or entrusted to the temple, and lending money from the treasury of the temple. The temple also had certain privileges. For example, anyone who seeked shelter in the temple enjoyed immunity (right of asylum). Therefore, people often took refuge in the sacred area surrounding the temple. During the time of Alexander, the sacred area and the borders of the refuge were enlarged, and King Mithridates enlarged this area even more, so that the sacred area stretched as far as the spot where an arrow shot from the pediment of the temple would land. Emperor Marcus Antonius, inspired by what Julius Caesar had done in Didyma, doubled this sacred area which thus included a section of the city too. Citizens critical of the fact that many criminals took refuge here and in other temples in the Empire, requested that the right asylum be lifted. In 22, Emperor Tiberius discussed the issue with the representatives of other famous temples, yet, the Temple of Artemis continued to serve as a refuge.

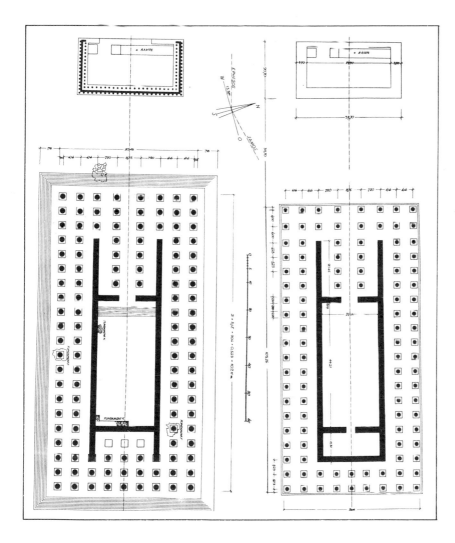

17- Plans of the Archaic Artemision and the Hellenistic temple.

The Archaic Artemision:

Strabo notes that the temple was destroyed and rebuilt seven times, and that even in those days it was considered one of the seven wonders of the world. Although the temple was located by the sea in antiquity, today, it is found 5 km. inland, on the right of the Selçuk-Kuşadası road. So far, excavations have revealed only for phases of construction. The oldest relics found were dated to the 7th century B.C.. They are pieces of bowls decorated with geometric designs, decorative gold objects and a group of ivory objects. The temple which is as old as these objects, was probably destroyed by the Cimmerians.

Just before 570 B.C., the architects Rhoichos and Theodoros completed the construction of the Temple of Hera in Samos. The popularity of this new temple must have encouraged the Ephesians to build a more magnificent temple than the Temple of Hera in the rival city of Samos. They engaged the architect Chersiphon and his son Metagenes of Knossos, and also invited Theodoros, because the area chosen as the site of the temple was swampy ground, like the location of the Temple of Hera. Also, they might have wanted their new temple to be similar to the Temple of Hera. The guest architects placed a layer of coal under the foundation, covered it with leather, and created a splendid temple measuring 55.10 metres by 115.14 metres. It is evident that the Cretan architects were quite familiar with Egyptian, Hittite and Assyrian architecture. The temple was the largest structure ever built of marble. The temple had a dipteral plan. On all four sides it had two rows of columns. Each column was 19 metres high and measured 1.21 metres in diameter. Using a double row of columns instead of a single row, gave it a wider appearance, yet cut down on its length. Pliny stated that there were a total of 127 columns. This forest of columns created an ideal setting, suitable for the goddess.

The number of rows of columns in the front and the back of the temple was disputed for many years, but recently it has been established that there were two rows of columns, both in the front and the back of the edifice. Pliny, who lived in the 1st century, stated that the thirty-six columns in the front had reliefs on them. What he had seen was undoubtedly a Hellenistic temple. If we assume that the temple was constructed on the foundation of a previous structure, and that Pliny based his remarks on older sources, then we can accept Pliny's statements about the temple. The reliefs on the thirty-six columns called columnae caelatae were located just below the capitals. The columnae caelatae were presented by the King of Lydia,

18- Western facade of the Temple of Artemis.

19- The City Walls. 3rd century B.C.

Croesus. One of these, which is in the British Museum, bears the inscription "presented by Croesus". Herodotus, too, stated that the inscription was true. It has been calculated that the architraves supported by the columns weighed twenty-four tons. Considering the equipment available then, it is difficult to comprehend how such heavy pieces could be lifted twenty metres and placed on the columns. The people believed that Artemis herself came and placed the architrave on the clomuns. No evidence has been found yet indicating the shape of the roof of the temple or how it was covered.

After the Cimmerian attacks, the old altar in front of the temple was rebuilt with stairs. Many votive offerings made of gold, ivory, electron silver and baked clay, as well as many electron silver coins were unearthed near the temple. These coins are the first minted money. Pythagoras, the tyrant of Ephesus, enlarged the altar after consulting the Delphic oracle about the recovery of his daughter who had unexpectedly become mute.

The Hellenistic Temple:

When a mentally unstable man named Herostratos who wanted a place in history, burned the temple in 356 B.C. on the night Alexander was born, the Ephesians decided to build a more magnificent temple. When Alexander came to Ephesus, the temple had not yet been completed. Although he wanted to assume all the past and future expenses of the construction of the new temple, the Ephesians did not accept his offer. The Hellenistic temple was situated on a podium ascended by a crepis of thirteen steps, and it measured 105 metres in length and 55 metres in width. The columns were 17.65 metres high. The plan of the archaic temple was not changed, and the columns in the front, as in the archaic temple, were ornamented with reliefs. Both Pliny and Vitrivius state that the reliefs on one of the columns were created by the famous sculptor Scopas. It is assumed that the sculptor Praxiteles had worked on the altar of the temple. The altar has a cornered 'U' plan and it is located in front of the temple. It has two rows of slim and tall Ionic columns, and at the two corners in the back, there are statues of quadrigas.

On one of the columnae caelatae in the British Museum, there is a relief depicting Akestis who had volunteered to be sacrificed in order to save the life of her husband. The woman in front of Hermes who is depicted naked, is Alkestis, and the winged figure is Thanatos (death). In the 5th century B.C., a competition called the "Amazon Statue Competition" was held among the famous sculptors of the time, to choose the statue to be placed in the temple. According to Pliny, the most famous sculptors antiquity, like Phidias, Polykleitos, Kresilas and Pharadmon entered the competition. At the end of the competition, the sculptors themselves were asked to choose the best statue. Each sculptor named his creation the best and the Polykleitos statue as the second best. Hence, the statue created by Polykleitos won the competition and was placed in the temple. There are many Roman copies of the statue in museums all over the world. It is still not known definitely which one of these statues is the original one created by Polykleitos. The temple of Artemis was destroyed for the last time by the attacks of Goths in 125 A.D.. Although Christianity was partially spread in the area, the temple was reconstructed but it did not last long. Later, when it was destroyed, most of its architectural elements were used in the construction of the Church of St. John. Upon the orders of Emperor Justinian, some of the architectural elements were used in the construction of Hagia Sophia. Today, there is not much left of the Temple of Artemis to indicate its magnificence. The excavations being carried out by Dr. A. Bammer of the Austrian Archaeological Institute, have unearthed very valuable finds which have added new dimensions to archaeology.

2. THE CITY WALLS AND THE MAGNESIA GATE

According to Strabo, the city walls were built by Lysimachos in the 3rd century B.C.. They are the best example of walls built during the Hellenistic period, both from the defence point of view and the excellent workmanship they exhibit. Certain sections of the wall on the flat ground are missing, but the sections on the mountain are very well-preserved. Toward the sea in the west, the height of the walls decreases in accordance with the natural slope of the mountain. The walls reach a tower located on a small hill visible from everywhere in Ephesus. The tower called St. Paul's Prison is different from the other towers on the wall. The partitions inside and its second storey give the tower an appearance of a jail. An inscription found inside records the name "Astyages Hill". To whom this name belongs is not known.

There are two important gates in the walls that give access to the city. One of them is the Koressos Gate located between the Stadium and the Vedius Gymnasium, and it is often mentioned in the inscriptions. This gate has not yet been excavated. The other gate is called the Magnesia Gate. It is on the Virgin Mary Road and still being excavated. The gate was built in the 3rd century B.C. together with the city walls, but during the reign of Emperor Vespasian (69-79), it was remodelled and turned into an arched ceremonial gate with three entrances.

The Hellenistic gate had a tall rectangular tower on each side and a courtyard behind it. Entrance into the city was through another gate located at the back of the courtyard. The square in front of the courtyard and the gate, are paved by large grey blocks of stone. Marble sarcophagi assumed to have belonged to important people were found in the square in front of the gate. The large aqueduct seen along the western side was routed through here long after the reign of Emperor Vespasian.

A branch of the road leaving the Magnesia Gate extends to the city of Magnesia, 30 km. south-east of Ephesus. The other branch encircles Panayır Dağı and reaches the Temple of Artemis. From here it goes through Ephesus and returns to the Magnesia Gate. The road was repaired by the Ephesian sophist Daminaus in the 2nd century.

All the streets and avenues in Ephesus were built according to the "right-angled" plan of the architect Hippodamos of Miletus. The streets and avenues were perpendicular to each other, but the road mentioned above was an exception. Excavations proved that the road existed during the Archaic period. Therefore, we can safely state that the road leading to the Temple of Artemis maintained its "sacred road" status throughout every age (Wood discovered the site of the Temple of Artemis by following this road).

20- Relics from the Artemision. Gold. 7th century B.C.

21- A bust. Marble. 3rd
century A.D.

22-Artemis Ephesia. Marble.
1st century A.D.

23- Fragment of the sarcophagus
at the Pursuit Gate.
2nd century A.D.

3. THE EASTERN GYMNASIUM

The remains seen to the north of the Magnesia Gate belonged to a large gymnasium. It was planned in accordance with the sacred road which passed in front of it, and was built in the 2nd century by the sophist Flavius Damianus during the repairing of the sacred road.

During antiquity, gymnasiums were centres for education and sport, similar to the boarding schools of our time. Generally, children between the ages of 6 to 16 attended the gymnasiums to study mathematics, music, oratory and physical education. The talented ones continued their education beyond the age of sixteen.

The Eastern Gymnasium which is one of the monumental structures in Ephsus, is a large complex consisting of a bath, a paleistra (sports arena), a courtyard, classrooms and imperial rooms. The propylon (entrance gate building) at the entrance on the eastern facade has four columns and a triangular pediment. Stores with a row of columns in the front were located on both sides of the propylon. The statues of Damianus and his wife Vedia Phaedrina were discovered in the course of excavations carried on here. They are exhibited in the İzmir Archaeological Museum.

Before reaching the parking lot, on the left of the road from the gymnasium, there are the remains of a circular structure 16 metres in diameter. Because of the signs of the Cross seen on the marble plates that cover this well-preserved structure, it was erroneously called the Tomb of St. Luke, whereas, the signs were carved on the plates long after the construction of the structure which had been built in the 1st century B.C., almost one hundred years before St. Luke.

24- The Eastern Gymnasium. 2nd century A.D.. F. Miltner.

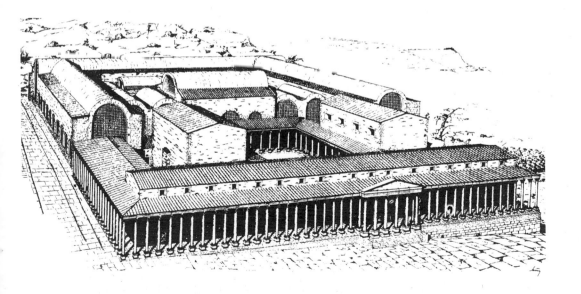

4. THE VARIUS BATHS

Although the Varius Baths were excavated intermittently between 1929 and 1979, they have not been completely unearthed. The structure was built at the foot of Pınar Dağı where the slope was flattened by the removal of soil. Thus, the building rested against the mountain, and the smoothed natural rocks served as walls. As seen in all the other Roman baths, the Varius Baths consisted of a frigidarium (cold room), a tepidarium (lukewarm room), a caldarium (hot room) and large accessory rooms. The walls are made of large blocks and the roof is made of brick and is vaulted. The latrine (toilet) is located at the southern side of the structure. It was altered and had new sections added at various times during the Roman and Byzantine periods. For example, the room in the south paved with mosaic was added on in the 5th century.

According to an inscription, both P. Flavius and his wife financed the construction of a hall in the baths.

5. THE AQUEDUCTS AND THE FOUNTAIN

In the course of excavations in Ephesus, many fountains belonging to different periods were unearthed. The springs which supplied water to the houses and the fountains were far from the city. Wells and cisterns also supplied water to the city.

The springs at Keltepe and Kenchiros (Değirmendere) located south of Kuşadası, are 42.5 km. from Ephesus. Following a route which runs by the westren foot of Bülbül Dağı, two ducts built of stone blocks bring water to Ephesus. One of these is 0.8 metre wide and 0.9 metre high, and the other is 0.65 metre wide and 0.45 metre high. The water runs at a rate of 61 litres per second.

The Klaseas (Pranga) Spring on the road to İzmir is another source. The water from here was brought to St. John Hill by a duct 10 km. long. The duct was built like an open canal, either carved into the rocks or supported by stone walls. These stone walls formed arches in certain places. Here, the water runs at a rate of 9 litres per second. Water to the Temple of Artemis was brought from the Selinus Spring in Şirince Köy. The 8 km. long aqueduct stretches all the way to the Artemision. During the excavations at the Artemision, thick lead pipes were discovered, and one of these is on display in the Ephesus Museum.

The source of water of the large Fountain located by the side of the street to the south of the Agora, is the spring known today as the Marnas Suyu (Spring) which is still quite popular. Remains of the aqueduct called Sextilius Pollio Duct, seen at the 6th kilometre of the Selçuk-Aydın road belongs to this spring. The water runs at a rate of 4.2 litres per second.

The Nympheum was constructed between the years 4 and 14 A.D. and it was planned in accordance with the street in front of it. Later, it was modified many times and attained its final form in the 4th century. During this period the facade of the fountain was decorated with statues of emperors and distinguished Ephesians.

25- Statue of a Nike. Marble. 1st century A.D

26-Earthenware water pipe from the Artemision. 2nd century A.D.

6. THE STATE AGORA

The area in front of the Fountain is the Stage Agora of Ephesus. It was built in the 1st century and measured 160 by 56 metres. It was a semi-sacred area where political and religious meetings were held under the supervision of the state. As in many other agoras, there is a rectangular temple in the middle (no. 13 on plan). The temple is almost completely destroyed. Its architectural elements were used in the construction of other structures in modern times. The discovery of structures related to water, led the archaeologists to believe first, that this was the Temple of Isis. Later it was suggested that it could be the Temple of Augustus. The group statue depicting one of the adventures of Odyseus with Polyphemus, originally decorated the pediment of the temple. Later it was placed by the pool of the Pollio Fountain situated to the west of the Agora. This group statue was discovered here and moved to Ephesus Museum where it is displayed in the Hall of the Fountain Relics. The temple was built in the 1st century B.C.

Excavations carried out at the State Agora unearthed the remains of the Archaic sacred road which encircles Panayır Dağı, and on both sides of the road are sarcophagi made of baked clay called Klazomenai type. The Agora attained its final shape during the reign of Emperor Theodosius (379-395). There used to be a stoa (collonade) both to the north and south of the Agora.

27- A general view of the State Agora. Late 1st century B.C.

*28- Rearrangement of
the pediment of the Temple
of Augustus. 1st
century B.C.*

7. THE BASILICA

The northern stoa of the Agora during the late Augustus period, was turned into a basilica 160 metres long. The Basilica had a wooden roof and three naves which were separated by two rows of columns. During the reign of Augustus, the column capitals were Ionic in style with bull heads decorating them, but during the renovations which took place in the late Empire period, they were turned into Corinthian style capitals. Excavations have revealed that the stoa on which the Basilica was built, is 1.30 metres below the ground. There were three entrances into the Basilica from another small stoa located between the Varius Baths and the Basilica. This stoa was modified during the Byzantine era and has lost its originality. The statues of Augustus and his wife that are displayed in the Ephesus Museum were discovered in this stoa.

*30- The Basilica. Early
1st century A.D.*

8. THE ODEION

Located to the north of the Agora, the Odeion resembles a small theatre. Therefore, it is also known as the Small Theatre. According to an inscription unearthed, it was built as a bouleuterion (council chamber) around 150 by Publius Vedius Antonius and his wife Flavia Papiana. They were members of a distinguished family in Ephesus.

Built on the slopes of Panayır Dağı, the structure consists of three main sections which are found in all other theatres: the cavea (auditorium), the orchestra (place of action for the actors) and the skene (the stage building). The semicircular cavea is divided into two by a diazoma (horizontal passage separating the rows of seats) in the centre. The marble seats exhibit quality craftsmanship. Most probably, the skene was two-storeyed. There is a narrow marble podium just in front of the skene where five doors open onto the podium. The door in the middle is taller and wider than the others. The orchestra is semicircular. The fact that there are no gutters for rain water in the centre of the orchestra indicates that the Odeion was roofed.

The Odeion seated 1,400. Spectators entered either through the paradoses (side entrances between the stage and auditorium), or through the galleries which were reached by the vaulted roofed staircases at the entrance of the paradoses.

The structure was used as an odeon during concerts and as a bouleterion during the meetings of the boule.

31. The State Agora and the Odeion.

32- The Odeion. 2nd century A.D.

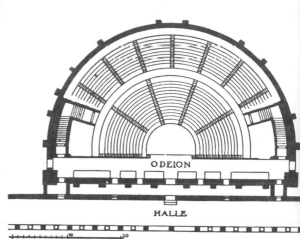

33- Entrance of the Odeion

ODEION

HALLE

35- The Odeion. 1st century A.D.

34- The Prytaneion Temples
of Dea Roma and D.J. Caesar

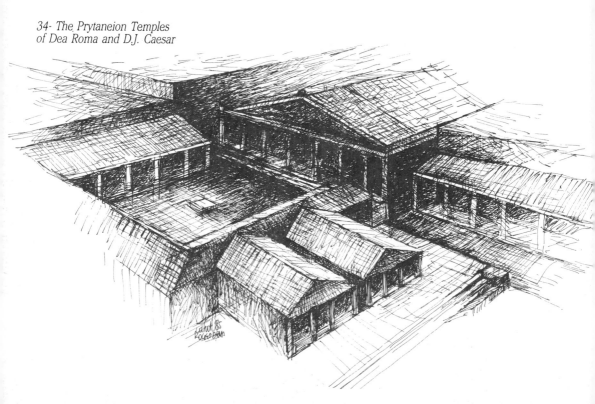

9. THE IMPERIAL CULT AND TEMPLES

36. The Artemision.

The Temples of Dea Roma and Divus Julius Caesar:

Complying with the wishes of Asians who were used to an imperial cult, Augustus gave permission for the establishment of an Augustus cult in Nikomedia for the Bithynian province, and in Pergamum for the Asian province, on the condition that the cults would be established jointly with the Roman goddess Dea Roma who already had a cult in Pergamum. These cults were founded for the non-Roman citizens of these provinces. For the Roman citizens living in both of these provinces, the cult of his adoptive father, Divus Julius (Caesar) who had been deified by the decision of the Senate, and the cult of Dea Roma, were to be established in Nikaia and Ephesus.

During the Roman Empire, being a Neokoros (an owner or a warden of an imperial temple) was very prestigious. Ephesus acquired its first imperial temple quite late during the reign of Emperor Domitian (81-96). When the neokoroship which they had attained by overcoming many obstacles, was in jeopardy after the death of Emperor Domitian, the Ephesians, thinking they would lose their prestige among their rivals, the Pergamese and the Smyians, dedicated the Temple of Domitian to his father, Vespasian, who had been deified.

Permission for the construction of the second imperial temple in Ephesus was given by Emperor Hadrian. The Ephesians obtained the permission

37- The Artemision.
E. Falkner.

when Hadrian came to Ephesus from Athens under the name of Zeus Olympus in 128 A.D..

Permission for the construction of the third temple was granted when Caracalla shared the throne with his brother Geta between 211 and 212. In 212, Caracalla killed his brother with his own hands. As mentioned in a letter Caracalla wrote to the Ephesians, he abandoned the idea of building this temple for the benefit of Artemis. The neokoroship which had been thus lost, was regained during the reign of Emperor Elagabalus (218-222).

The records of the Roman Senate indicate that permission to build the fourth royal temple in Ephesus was granted during the reign of Emperor Valerian (251-260).

The possession of an imperial temple was a matter of great prestige among the cities in the Asian province. Ephesians made every effort and spent a lot of money in order not to lose the Proteia (the first place), especial-

38- Eros on a Dolphin. Bronze. 2nd century A.D.

ly to Pergamum and Smyrna.

The imperial temples were administered by high priests called Archeireus, who added the name of the city where their temple was located to the beginning of their titles. Even though the temples were owned by the cities, they were respected by every citizen in the province. The exact relationship between the archiereis and the asiarchs who were the chief archiereis in the province is not known. Asiarch may also mean the organizer and the director of semi-religious plays called Koina Asias, which were organized in a different province every four years to honour the emperor. Being an archiereus, above all, was an honourable duty requiring financial sacrifices.

Gladiators and wild animal fights were closely associated with imperial cults and their celebrations. Although the Asians did not like these types of games much, during the Roman Empire, the games gained some popularity among the Asians.

Rich families in Ephesus, like the Vediuses, established special gladiator schools for these types of games. Inscriptions praising the asiarchs mention that they spent a lot of money on these games. The imperial cult never became a true religion. Its aim was to create and secure unity among the peoples living within the borders of the Roman Empire without discriminating against language, culture and religion. The temples of Dea Roma and Divus Julius Caesar are located just to the west of the Odeien,

39- Head of Young Dionysus. 2nd century A.D.

in the middle of a courtyard surrounded by a columned potico.

These small temples had four columns on their eastern facade. Since other structures had been built on them, they are in ruins. Today, only the marble walls of the podiums which exhibit exquisite craftsmanship, and the walls of their foundations are extant.

When Emperor Augustus came to Ephesus in 29 B.C., he gave permission for the construction of these temples. Upon completion between the years 4 and 14 A.D., one of these was dedicated to the Roman goddess Dea Roma and the other to Divus Julius Caesar, the adoptive father of Augustus.

10. THE OFFICIAL ESTABLISHMENTS OF THE CITY AND THE PRYTANEION

During the Roman Empire, Ephesus maintained its 'free city' (civitas libera) status. All the official duties relating to the administration of the city were honorary.

The rich Ephesians subsidized official expenses, such as the expenses that were incurred during important festivals and celebrations, and also for the construction and restoration of the official buildings. Also, rich Ephesians competed for the honour and fame attached to such functions, and as a reward, monuments dedicated to them were erected on main streets or at the Agoras.

The political system in the city involved two groups. One of these was called the Boule and it was the advisory assembly. It consisted of three hundred members called Bouleutes and the assembly met in the Odeion. The other group was called Demos i.e. "people's assembly" and consisted of all the Ephesians. They met in the Theatre. Each assembly had a secretary called Boule Grammateus and Demos Grammateus respectively, who were in charge of administrative services. The Demos Grammateus also served as the president of the city administration. When Ephesus was a Polis (a city state), a Strategos was in charge of security in the city. During the Empire, this function attained an administrative status.

Eirenarchs and Paraphylakes served as the police and security officials in the city. Agoranomoi were in charge of order in the Agora and made sure that the amount of grain was adequate and that it was marketed in an orderly manner.

Ephesus owed its wealth and fame to its harbour where Limenarchs were in charge.

The highest religious and administrative duty in the city was the prytany, which could be assumed both by men and women. The duty of the prytanis who belonged to a distinguished class of people in the city, was to make sure that the eternal flame in the city's hearth, located in the Prytaneion, never went out. The flame symbolized the existence of the city and the hearths in all the houses in Ephesus. In the name of Hestia, the goddess of the hearth, the prytanis assumed the job with great pleasure. The prytanis also supervised all the cults in the city and made sure that daily sacrifices were carried out. The expenses incurred were paid by the prytanis.

Throughout its history, the organization and administration of the Temple of Artemis were independent of the administration of the city. The Prytaneion of Ephesus is located at the western end of the Basilica. Besides the accessory buildings, it consists of a courtyard surrounded by a portico in the front and a large covered hall behind it. With its eight tall and thick Doric columns in the facade, it resembles a large temple. Two of the columns were repaired and placed in their original locations. The interior of the Prytaneion, in accordance with its exterior appearance, is quite ornate. In each of the four corners of the hall there are double columns with heart-shaped cuts. The foundation of the altar made of basalt, is seen in the centre of the hall. The eternal flame of Ephesus burned day and night for centuries, in this hall called Hestia's Sacred Area. The Artemis statues displayed in the Ephesus Museum, were found in this area in an excellent state of preservation. Some of the inscriptions found on the columns and on the architectural fragments spread over the area give the list of the "League of Curetes". The Curetes were a class of priests in the Artemision. Originally there were six of them, but later their number was increased to nine. The league of Curetes which used to be affiliated only with the Artemision during the Classic and Hellenistic periods, acquired a place in the Prytaneion with Emperor Augustus. Thus, most of the lists of the Curetes were

40- The temples of Dea Roma and D.J. Caesar. 1st century A.D.

41- The Prytaneion. Columns with inscriptions. 1st century A.D.

42- A general view of the Sacred Road. Roman Period.

discovered in the Prytaneion. The main function of the league was to celebrate the birth of Ephesian Artemis in Ortygia, near Ephesus, every year.

The Prytaneion was constructed in the 3rd century B.C. and attained its final shape during the reign of Emperor Augustus. After it was destroyed for various reasons, its columns and some of its other architectural elements were used in the construction of the Scholastikia Baths. In the course of excavations they were brought back to the Prytaneion. On each side of the road which runs between the Prytaneion and Domitian Square, there is a statue base with figures on it. The base on the left bears a figure of the god Hermes depicted nude, and holding a ram by its horns with one hand and a caduceus, his symbol, with the other hand. On the other side of the base, a tripod with a snake between its legs is depicted. The base on the right also bears the figure of a nude Hermes holding a goat by its horns, and on the other side of the base there is a tripod with a plate between its legs.

43- Statue-base with a relief of Hermes. Marble. 3rd century A.D..

11. THE MEMMIUS MONUMENT

44- The Memmius Monument. 1st century B.C..

Located on the north side of Domitian Square, the Memmius Monuments resembles a four sided victory arch. Its base is made of convex local stones and the other sides are made of marble. A crepis of four steps surrounds it. On each facade, there are semicircular niches connected to each other by arches on which there are blocks bearing figures. Most of the blocks with figures are missing. The figures resembling soldiers wearing helmest belong to Memmius, his father Caicus, and his grandfather Sulla, the dictator.

The Latin inscription found on a piece of the architrave at the eastern end of the structure states "Caius Memmius, the saviour, is the son of Caicus, grandson of Cornelius Sulla."

The monument was built in the 1st century B.C.

12. THE FOUNTAIN

45- The Round Structure 1st century B.C..

There is a fountain to the west of the Caicus Memmius Monument. It has a long and narrow (rectangular) pool, and on the walls of the pool there are four Corinthian columns. The pool consists of three sections and the middle section is wider than the rest. The wall behind this section is semicircular and water ran through here into the pool. In front of the pool, there were four bases, but only the foundation of two are still visible today. Statues of the four emperors; Diocletian, Maximian, Constantius Chlorus and Galerius, who shared the throne between 293 and 305, were located on the bases. The statues were placed here during the construction of the fountain to display the unity among the emperors. The statues of the same emperors used to be in front of the Temple of Hadrian also.

The western side of Domitian Square has not been excavated yet. The round monument in the centre of the square was brought here from another part of the city in the 4th century. The exterior of the monument is decorated with a garland carried on bulls' heads. Right next to this, there is a relief of a flying Nike holding a wreath. This triangular architectural element belongs to the Heracles Gate located at the beginning of Curetes Street.

A narrow street paved with marble blocks like all the other streets in Ephesus, leads south from the square. On the side of the street where the Agora is, there are storerooms and two-storeyed structures used for various services. The architectural fragments seen in the middle of the square belong to these buildings.

46- The Flying Nike. Marble. 2nd century A.D..

13. THE POLLIO FOUNTAIN

This is located to the east of Domitian Square, next to the western side of the Agora. With its wide and high arch which supports the triangular pediment and its small pool, it is quite an appealing structure. Water fell into the pool through the semicircular apsidal wall on the side of the Agora. The Polyphemus group statue, which today is exhibited in the Ephesus Mesum, was found in the pool on a pedestal built to fit the apsidal wall. These statues were originally on the pediment of the Temple of Isis in the middle of the Agora, but after the collapse of that structure, they were brought here. The theme of the group statue is one of the adventures of Odysseus in the Aegean following the Trojan wars, specifically, his adventure with Polyphemos, son of Posseidon. According to an inscription, the fountain was constructed by Sextilius Pollio in 97 A.D.

48- The Pollio Fountain.
Early 1st century B.C.

47- Head of Dionysus.
3rd century A.D.

14. THE TEMPLE OF DOMITIAN

During its history, Ephesus was granted the right to be a neokoros four times. In antiquity, being a neokoros was considered a very honourable privilege which every city yearned for.

Ephesus was granted the temple wardenship for the first time by Emperor Domitian (81-96). The temple dedicated to him was built on a terrace measuring 50 by 100 metres on the south side of Domitian Square. Not much is left of the temple. Our information on the structure comes from the remains of its foundation. The podium on which the temple was erected measured 24 by 34 metres, and it was surrounded by an eight-stepped crepis. Apparently, the temple was a small prostyle (a temple preceded by a porch with columns) and had eight columns on the short sides and thirteen columns on the long sides. Also, in front of the cella which measured 9 by 17 metres, there were four columns. The altar was located 10 metres in front of the cella and had a cornered "U" shaped plan and steps leading up to it. A section of the altar displaying exquisite craftsmanship is now exhibited in the Ephesus Museum. In order to show their gratitude to the emperor, the Ephesians erected his 5 metres-tall statue in the temple. Some of the parts of the statue, which measured seven metres in height including its base, are displayed in the Ephesus Museum, and the head of the statue which is in good condition, is on display in the Izmir Archaeological Museum.

There was a row of storerooms to the west of the terrace on which the temple was situated and on the side facing the square. There is a parapet consisting of two tiers of columns. There are reliefs on the columns of the upper row. Two of these columns were discovered in another part of the city and brought back to their original location.

After the Emperor Domitian was assassinated by one of his servants, the temple wardenship which the Ephesians had acquired with great pains, was in jeopardy. In order not to lose it, the Ephesians deified the emperor's father, Vespasian, and dedicated the temple to him.

49- The Temple of Domitian. 81-96 A.D.

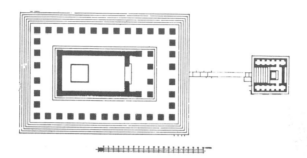

50-Entrance of the Temple of Domitian.

51 - The columned parapet in front of the Temple of Domitian.

15. THE INSCRIPTION GALLERY

The inscriptions relating to the history of Ephesus are displayed in the substructure at the eastern end of the terrace of the Domitian Temple. More than two thousand inscriptions have been discovered either by chance or during excavations. From these inscriptions, we have learned about the People's Assembly, Senate decisions, appraisals and punishments, and decrees of emperors and kings.

Only some of the exemplary inscriptions are displayed according to subject and chronology. The texts and their interpretations have been translated and displayed next to the inscriptions.

The oldest inscriptions discovered in Ephesus are dated to the 7th century B.C. The preserved sections of these inscriptions displayed as nos. 1 and 2 give no indication about the theme or the purpose of the text. As in all the inscriptions of the Archaic period, the position of the letters in each line were in register with the previous line, and words were separated from each other by a period.

In the inscriptions numbered 4, the death penalty requested for a religious crime is described. In the text, the Proegors (the state attorneys) state the names of forty-four or forty-six people who treated a group of ambassadors badly, and looted the gifts they were either taking to or had taken from the Temple of Artemis in Sardes, and request the death penalty for them.

The inscription numbered 11 belongs to the 4th and 3rd centuries B.C. It states "up to the roof, this wall is the common property of Moskhion and Eucleides", and therefore indicates common property law.

52- The Inscription Gallery (the cryptoportico of the Temple of Domitian.

53-The Milestone
between Ephesus and Sardes.
Roman Period.

54- A bust. Marble
3rd century A.D.

55- Head of Tyche.
From the frontal of the
Temple of Hadrian.

The inscription numbered 13 is an appraisal of an Ephesian tutor serving in the Pergamese Palace. It was written by King Attalos II to the Ephesian People's and Advisory Assemblies. A tutor named Aristo had educated the future King of Pergamum, Attalos III, and since King Attalos II was quite pleased by the services of Aristo, he declared his pleasure to the Ephesians. The inscription is dated to 155 B.C..

The text of inscriptions numbered 14-26 honour different people. Number 20 states that the famous sophist Titus Flavius Damian, between 166-167 A.D. donated 22000 medimmes (a measure of grain) to the retreating Roman armies following the Parthian wars, built a new hall in the Varius Baths, donated 19,816 denarii of his own money to the city, and therefore was honoured by the Trade Guild of the Agora.

Number 26 states that an Ephesian athlete, whose name cannot be read, was honoured for his victories in the thirteen cities of southern Italy, Asia, Greece and the Islands.

In number 27, the decrees about the procedures to be carried out by the Prytanis relating to sacrifices, are listed. It is evident from this inscription dated to the 3rd century, that Prytany was a very expensive duty. The prytanis was not only the high priest of Hestia, the goddess of the sacred hearth in the Prytaneion, but also was in charge of all the cults in the city.

Inscription number 31 is about Emperor Hadrian who came to Ephesus from Athens in 128 under the name of Zeus Olympios and states: it is dedicated to the goddess of destiny who rules well. To Zeus Olympios, father of the land "to Emperor Caesar Traianus Hadrianus Augustus, the saviour of the city and its adoptive founder".

16. THE GAIUS LAECANIUS BASSUS FOUNTAIN

This is located on the corner where the road from the south of the Agora and the road from Domitian Square intersect each other. The Gaius Laecanius Bassus Fountain, which is one of the monumental fountains in Ephesus, was built in the direction of the Temple of Domitian. It consists of a courtyard, two tiers of columns on all three sides and two pools in the front. It also has a large pediment on the facade. The pediment is at a height of 9 metres. In each tier the columns are arranged in pairs. On the facade there are 20 and on each side there are 14 columns. There were statues in the niches with frontals located between two columns. The statues of Triton, the Nymphs and Muses, which were discovered during excavations, are on display in the Hall of the Fountain Relics, in the Ephesus Museum.

According to an inscription, the fountain was built between 75-80 by Gaius Laecanius Bassus, one of the governors of the Asian province.

*56- A Nymph. Marble.
Late 1st century A.D.*

17. THE HERACLES GATE

The gate is located at the beginning of Curetes Street which stretches westward from the Memmius Monument. It is a two-storeyed edifice. In the lower storey there is a wide arched passageway, and in the upper storey there are six columns in a row. Reliefs of flying Nikes that are found today in Domitian Square, used to be situated at the corners where the arch joins the pillars with Corinthian capitals. One of these reliefs and most of the construction fragments have not been found yet.

The two centrally located columns at the upper level look like the lintels of the gate. On these two columns, there are two reliefs of Heracles depicted wrapped in a Nemea lion skin. They are like the caryatids supporting Corinthian capitals and exhibit 2nd century craftsmanship. They were moved here in the 5th century from another location.

18. THE CURETES STREET

57- Curetes Street. Roman Period.

In mythology, the Curetes were known as semi-deities. Later "Curetes" referred to a class of priests in Ephesus. The collegium they founded was considered the largest cult in Ephesus. Many inscriptions about the Curetes were discovered in different locations in Ephesus, especially at the Prytaneion. First, there were six of them, but later their number was increased to nine. The aim of this group was to recreate the birth of Artemis Ephesia in Ortygia, near Ephesus. According to mythology, while Leto, impregnated by Zeus, was giving birth to the twins, Artemis and Apollo, Curetes made a lot of noise with their weapons so that Zeus' wife Hera who was jealous of Leto, would be confused and not see the birth of the twins.

In the beginning, the Curetes were affiliated only with the Artemision, but during the Roman Empire they acquired a place in the Prytaneion also. They were chosen every year.

The street named after the Curetes stretches from the Heracles Gate to the Celsus Library, and since it is located in the centre of the city, there are many monumental structures facing the street. Covered columned galleries paved with mosaics occupy both sides of the street. The doors of the storerooms, houses and other buildings opened onto these galleries. The statues of the benefactors of the city were situated on the bases seen in front of the columns. Some of these bases have inscriptions. One of these statues was discovered near the Heracles Gate and it belonged to the physician Alexandros. The statue of Consul Stephanos which is now in the Ephesus Museum, was also discovered on this street.

In the middle of the 4th century, earthquakes destroyed the street and rendered it unusable. After the last earthquake, it was repaired, using columns and architectural elements brought from various locations in the city.

The storerooms that face the street were connected to the houses behind them.

19. THE TRAJAN FOUNTAIN

This is located at the north end of Curetes Street, and according to an inscription unearthed, it was constructed between 102 and 114 and dedicated to Emperor Trajan (98-117).

The dedicatory inscription is on a large cornice located today next to the fountain. At the facade of the fountain there is a pool in the centre, and there are two tiers of columns on three sides. Between the columns there are niches with statues. In the central niche, there used to be a statue

58- The Resting Warrior. 1st century A.D..

59- The Trajan Fountain. 97-117 A.D..

60- Artemis Ephesia. 1st century A.D..

of Emperor Trajan. Today, only the base and a piece of the foot of the statue are extant. Water ran into the pool from a wide channel under the statue of the Emperor. The fountain has been repaired, but decreased in size in order to give an idea about its general structure. Originally, it stood 12 metres high. The statues of Dionysus, a Satyr, Aphrodite, and members of the imperial family unearthed during the excavations, are now exhibited in the Ephesus Museum.

20. THE ROUND TOWER

The remains of a round tower can be seen behind the Trajan Fountain at the foot of Panayır Dağı. It was built around 50 as a monument and was situated on a rectangular podium. It consisted of a cylindrical structure in the centre, surrounded by a row of two-tiered columns. The lower columns are Doric and those above are Ionic in style. Only the podium of the tower is still standing.

Between the Trajan Fountain and The Scholastikia Baths, a street parallel to Marble Street runs northward. It is paved with marble slabs and has steps in places. The section of the street up to the Theatre has been excavated completely.

21. THE SCHOLASTIKIA BATHS

The three-storeyed structure (including the basement) is one of the largest buildings of its kind in Ephesus, and it is located on the north side of Curetes Street between the Trajan Fountain and the Temple of Hadrian. During the Roman Empire, the baths had their own regulations, and they were quite popular among both the poor and the rich. Certain baths were free to the poor so that they could enjoy them too. The rich preferred to visit the baths in the afternoon with their servants and stayed long. In the apodyterium, they used to disrobe; in the sudotorium they used to sweat; and in the caldarium, the servants used to massage and wash their masters. After bathing, they would talk about the affairs of the day and discuss politics and philosophy in the tepidarium. Before leaving the baths, they would swim and refresh themselves in the pool of the frigidarium.

61- C. Scholastikia who restored the Scholastikia Baths. 4th century A.D..

The baths lost their popularity after the Romans, and although they were completely forgotten by the Middle Ages, they were popularized again by the Seljuk and Ottoman Turks.

The Scholastikia Baths had two entrances; one from Curetes Street and the other from a street to the east. Both doors opened into the apodytreium which was a very large hall with columns and niches. The wall on the side of the "L" shaped street is apsidal. The statue of Christian Scholastikia who had the baths repaired in 400, is in one of the niches. The frigidarium was to the west of the apodyterium, and in the middle of it there was an eliptical cold water pool. The entrance of the tepidarium was through an arched door on the northern side of the apodyterium. Hot air circulated through earthenware pipes placed in the walls and under the floor. Right by the wall in the east, there is a small area paved with coloured marble mosaic, and it is a few centimetres lower than the surface. This area is the original floor covering of the baths.

In the course of renovations around 400, the original floor was recovered with marble slabs. A small, narrow door from the tepidarium led into the caldarium which is in an excellent state of preservation today. During renovations at different periods, its walls were covered with marble and brick plaques. Baked clay supports placed under the floor covering of the caldarium formed channels through which hot air circulated. The furnace (hypocaust) which supplied the hot air, is to the west of the caldarium.

The Scholastikia Baths were built in the 1st century and repaired many times until the end of the 4th century.

62- The Brothel and the Scholastikia Baths.

63- Caldarium of the
Scholastikia.

64- The Latrina (WC).
1st century A.D..

65- The southern
portico of Curetes
Street.

22. THE LATRINA

On the west side of the Scholastikia Baths, there is a narrow street with a vaulted covering. The door of the Latrina which was the public toilet of the city opens onto this street. In the centre of the structure there is a square pool, and a row of stone toilet bowls are located on the sides. In front of the stone toilets there is a water channel, and the floor of the Latrina is covered with mosaic. The pool is not covered but it is enclosed by walls. The four columns at the corners of the pool support the roof of the Latrina.

23. THE TEMPLE OF HADRIAN

This is one of the most attractive edifices on Curetes Street, and it must have been built at the latest by the year 138. The temple consists of a monumental pronaos (porch in front of a cella) and a small, bare cella (main chamber). In front of the facade of the pronaos, there are four columns with Corinthian capitals supporting a triangular pediment. Above the two columns in the middle, there is an arch which curves down from the pediment, and the bust of Tyche, the goddess of the city, which adorns the centre of the arch.

The lintel over the doors is richly decorated with classic motifs such as eggs or strands of pearls. On the second semicircular frontal over the door, the figure of a maiden resembling Medusa is depicted among flowers and acanthus leaves.

The original of the frieze found at the upper lintel of the door of the pronaos is now in the Ephesus Museum. During restoration, the original frieze was replaced by its plaster cast. The frieze consists of four sections. On the first three sections from the left, gods and goddesses with Androklos, the founder of Ephesus, chasing the boar; gods with Amazons; Amazons and a Dionysiac procession are depicted. The theme depicted on the fourth section is different from the others. Starting from left, Athena, Selena (the goddess of the moon), a man, Apollo, a female figure, Androklos, Heracles, father of Theodosius, Emperor Theodosius, Artemis Ephesia, wife and son of Theodosius, and the goddess Athena are depicted on the fourth section of the frieze. The temple was destroyed in an earthquake in the 4th century, and the fourth section of the frieze must have been brought here from another structure in Ephesus in the course of restorations following the earthquake. The dedicatory inscription on the architrave of the temple, states that the temple was dedicated by P. Quintilius to Emperor Hadrian around 138.

In front of the columns there are four bases with inscriptions, and the statues of the four emperors who shared the throne of the Roman Empire between 293-305. They are: Diocletian, Maximian, Constantius Chlorus, and Galerius, as indicated by the inscriptions on the bases.

66- The Temple of Hadrian. 2nd century A.D..

The excavation of the storerooms across from the Temple of Hadrian has been completed. Some of the storerooms were connected to the houses above them by a staircase. The houses were built on the slopes of Bülbül Dağı, so that each house served as the terrace of the next house on the slope. The narrow side street with steps between the houses, connected the houses to Curetes Street.

Since these houses were located in the centre of the city, they must have belonged to the distinguished citizens of Ephesus. This is why they are also referred to as 'houses of the rich' or 'palaces on the slopes'.

Each house had a door which opened onto the side street from a terrace and a peristyle (courtyard) surrounded by rooms. Most of these houses were three-storeyed, and the courtyards in the centre measured between 25-50 metres. The courtyard was surrounded by a colonade and paved with marble. The houses had running water. There was a fountain either in the peristyle or on the side of it, and some of the houses had either a cistern or a well. The peristyles were not covered, in order not to obstruct daylight, but since there were no windows, the rooms were dark anyway. Almost all of these houses were heated by the hypocaust system as used in the baths.

67- Fresco from one of the Houses on the Slope.

68- Houses on the Slope.

The floors were paved with mosaics and the walls were covered with frescoes or decorative marble. New frescoes were painted over the old ones, which were scraped so that the plaster of the new frescoes would hold. Generally, the frescoes depicted mythological themes, gods, goddesses, Muses, Eros and scenes from tragedies or comedies. Also, floral motifs were often used. The remains excavated, indicate that these houses on the slopes were constructed during the reign of Augustus, but were remodelled many times up until the 7th century. Toward the end of the 7th century, some of the houses which were filled with soil and rubble were used as grain depots. Many water mills were built on the houses and used for years.

Two of the houses have been restored and opened to the public. The household items unearthed during excavations are displayed on site.

Peristyle House I

The entrance is located at the end of the street with steps, across from the Temple of Hadrian. It has been restored to give a general idea about all the other houses. The two-storeyed house covers an area of 900 m², but since the second storey has collapsed completely, it is impossible to learn anything about it.

The house has twelve rooms used for various purposes. The few steps at the entrance lead down to a hall (A.1), the floor of which is covered with black and white mosaics. A staircase leading upstairs, and a fountain with an arch which was built later, are found on the right side of the hall. An arched passage straight across from the entrance leads into the peristyle (A.2). A Doric column is seen in each corner of the peristyle which is paved with marble. The remains of a fountain are seen on the north side of the peristyle. Floors of the rooms (numbered A.10-11) behind the fountain are covered with mosaics, and the walls are decorated with frescoes where red or red tones predominate. Although this house was built in the 1st century, these two rooms were added on around 400, during renovations. On the other side of the peristyle (courtyard) there is a vaulted niche (A.6) and also the remains of a staircase leading upstairs. Adjacent to the staircase there is another well-preserved room (A.7). The floors and the walls of this room are covered with mosaics and frescoes respectively. Although originally the room had been built as part of the room of the adjacent house, later it was separated from it.

To the west of the peristyle, there is a well-preserved hall (A.3) the walls of which are 4 metres high. Since the frescoes on each side of its entrance depict scenes from plays, the hall is called "the theatre". During the Roman period, the actors wore masks while acting, therefore, in the frescoes, the figures are depicted wearing masks. The scene on the right is from the play "Sikyonios" by Menander, who wrote comedies, and the one on the left is from the play "Orestes" by Euripides. On the wide walls of the "theatre" there are full-size figures of nude or seminude men and women.

One of these figures holds a plate. On the first section of the wall on the left there is a depiction of a mask, and next to it, there is a scene describing the fight between Heracles and Acheloos, the river god. The theme of the fresco is the following: "Acheloos, the most important river god in Western Greece, wanted to marry Deianira, daughter of the King of Calydon. Deianira was scared of Acheloos who could transform himself into a bull or a dragon, for example. She preferred to marry Heracles instead. Acheloos transformed himself into a dragon and fought Heracles". The floor of the "theatre" is covered with mosaics of geometric designs. These mosaics and frescoes date back to the 2nd century.

The bathroom is to the south of the vestibule (A.8). The foundation of the bathroom and its hypocaust are still extant, but the marble floor covering and the water ducts have been destroyed. In the hypocaust (space below the floor into which hot air was piped) there were baked clay supports which enabled the hot air to circulate. The kitchen (A.12) is adjacent to the bathroom. Smaller rooms and a service door which opens onto the street, are located next to the kitchen.

The objects displayed in this house were brought to light in the course of excavations.

69- Plan of the Houses on the Slope.

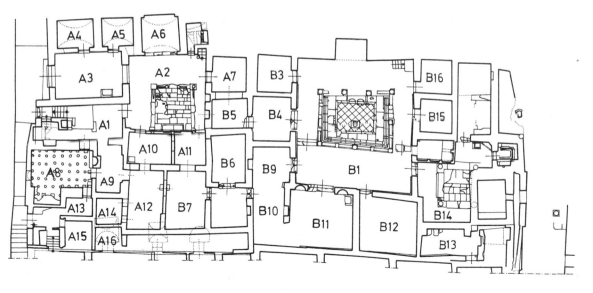

Peristyle House II

There is an access from the first house, to the second house which has two peristyles and is larger than the other. It was built in the 1st century, but modified and restored many times until the 6th century. The main peristyle (B.1) is in a better state of preservation and has elegant columns with Corinthian capitals. The columns seen on the south side of the peristyle consist of unmatched fragments and they were found in situ. These columns were erected in the course of alterations in the 5th century.

The long vestibule on the south side of the peristyle is paved with black and white mosaics of geometric design. Right across from this vestibule is the southern vestibule where the Triton and Nereid mosaic is found. Triton is depicted holding his father's symbol, the trident, in his left hand, and pulling the reins of hippocampus (sea horse) on which a semi-nude Nereid is riding, with his right hand. This vivid mosaic is seen in the vaulted niche (B.6) located on this side of the peristyle. The floor of the vaulted niche is covered with black and white marble of basket-weave design. The most beautiful mosaic seen in all the houses on the slopes covers the vault of this niche. The mosaic made of colourful small pieces of glass, covers the vault completely. In the centre, the heads of Dionysus and Ariadne are depicted in a circle, and around them there are trees and animals like peacocks, ducks and roosters. The mosaic belongs to the 5th century. On each side of the vault, there is a frieze bearing frescoes which depict Eros figures carrying is garland. Rooms of various sizes are located on the east side of the house. The floors of these rooms are paved with black and white mosaics, and the walls are covered with frescoes of birds and flowers.

On the walls of the rooms numbered B.9 and B.10, there are panels

71- Houses on the Slope. Peristyle House II.

70- A scene from "Orestes" by Euripides (fresco). From the Peristyle House 1. 2nd century.

of frescoes depicting standing Muses. These frescoes date back to the 4th century.

The rooms numbered B.11 and B.12 are dining rooms. The mosaics on the eastern wall of B.11 were repaired in modern times, using a single colour. The kitchen is located at the western corner of the peristyle and its walls are decorated with frescoes of fish and birds. The second peristyle, B.14, is located on the western side of the house. The lavatory which could serve more than one person at a time and its washstand, open onto this peristyle.

72- A scene from "Sikyonios" by Menander (fresco). From the Peristyle House I. 2nd century.

73- A Nereid, a Seahorse and Triton (mosaic). From the Peristyle House II. 2nd century.

74- Heracles and Acheloos Fighting (fresco). From the Peristyle House I. 2nd century.

*75- Houses on the slope.
A fresco from
the Peristyle House II.
2nd century A.D.*

25. THE OCTAGON

There is an octagonal mausoleum across from the Temple of Hadrian, right by the street. In Ephesus, the statues of those who organized competitions, donated money to the temples, or paid for the upkeep of official buildings to acquire honour and fame, were placed in special areas like the Agora or the main street. Also, inscriptions praising them and octagonal mausoleums dedicated to them, were erected at these special places.

This octagonal mausoleum situated on a rectangular base belonged to such a person. It is surrounded by a row of columns with Corinthian capitals and its roof is pyramidal. Both the eaves and the base are decorated with lotus, palm and acanthus leaves.

The sarcophagus made of andesite, is in a small room with low vaults. Entrance to the tomb is through a long and narrow passage (dromos) under the house behind it.

The Octagon which was built between 40-20 B.C. was unearthed in 1929. The skeleton in it belong to a young girl between the age of eighteen and twenty.

26. THE BYZANTINE FOUNTAIN

Next to the Octagon, there is a row of Greek and Latin inscriptions which state the decrees of emperors Valentinian I, Valens and Gratianus, pertaining to the restoration of the city and the city wall, following the disastrous earthquake around the middle of the 4th century, and holidays in the Asian province. Another mausoleum shaped like a horseshoe is seen after these inscriptions. Since a fountain was built on it in the 5th century, the tomb has partially collapsed.

The fountain consists of a pool in the front and the main building behind the pool. The walls of the fountain are decorated with signs of the Cross.

27. THE BROTHEL

The portico of Curetes Street which comes after the Temple of Hadrian, was turned into a Byzantine stoa (a long covered hall with columns in front) during the Byzantine era. Right behind it, there is a peristyle house known as the Brothel.

It was probably built between 98-117 during the reign of Emperor trajan. The Brothel, Public Lavatory and the Scholastikia Baths constitute a complex, and these buildings were restored in the 4th century. An inscription found in the lavatory indicated that it was a brothel. Its entrance is located on Marble Street and it has another door which opens onto Curetes Street.

The upper storey has been completely destroyed. The ground floor is quite spacious, and although the walls were once covered with frescoes, now only traces of them can be seen.

76- Priapos 1st century A.D..

The dining room (triclinium) is one of the rooms in the west, and there is a colourful mosaic depicting the four seasons on the floor. Adjacent to the dining room, there is a bath with hot and cold water. Also in the west, there is an eliptical pool, the floor of which is covered with mosaics. Although this section was damaged in the course of alterations near the pool in modern times, the mosaic is in good condition. The figures of three women drinking, a servant standing, a mouse eating food crumbs and a cat, are depicted in the coloured mosaic. A well which is still used today, is located on the side next to Curetes Street. The baked clay statue of Priapos with a huge phallus, which is displayed in the Ephesus Museum, was discovered in this well.

There is a small square on Curetes Street before it reaches the Celsus Library. From this square, Marble Street runs to the right and another road

---

28. THE MONUMENTAL GATE

77- The Monumental Gate (the Gate of Hadrian). 2nd century A.D..

runs to the left. The Monumental Gate is located at the beginning of this street and it faces the square. Since the street has not been excavated yet, we do not know to where is leads, but we can assume that it leads to an important religious building or a sacred area, since it starts with a monumental gate.

The gate was built in the beginning of the 2nd century. Only four pilasters (a support projecting from a wall) border, its three passages, and various fragments scattered in the vicinity are extant. The pilasters supported the columns with Ionic capitals. The columns were arranged in pairs, and there was an arch between the two columns in the middle. Above these, there were six Ionic columns also arranged in pairs but smaller than the lower ones. The pediment was just like the pediment of the Temple of Hadrian, and there was an arch between the two columns in the middle.

The gate must have been destroyed during an earthquake in the middle of the 4th century.

---

29. THE CELSUS LIBRARY

The Celsus Library, restoration of which has been completed, is one of the monumental edifices in Ephesus.

In 92, Tiberius Julius Celsus Polemaeanus was a consul in Rome, and was in charge of all the public buildings. Between either 105-106 or 106-107 he was the proconsul (governor) of the Asian province, the capital of which was Ephesus, When he died in 114 at the age of seventy his son Tiberius Julius Aquila, built the library as a heroon (mausoleum) for his father. It is assumed that the construction of the library was completed in 117.

The sarcophages of Celsus is located in a tomb under the apsidal wall in the library. The sarcophagus is made of high quality marble and decorated with figures of Eros, Nike, rosettes and garlands in relief. In 1904, the sarcophagus was opened during excavations, and a skeleton was discovered in another lead coffin in the sarcophagus.

The building reflects the characteristics of the age of Emperor Hadrian. The facade is two-storeyed. On the lower storey, the columns with Corinthian capitals are placed on a 21 metre long podium reached by nine steps. The columns are arranged in pairs, and between them there are three doors with richly decorated frames. The door in the middle is wider and taller than the other two.

Statues seen in the niches between the doors, are copies of the originals which were taken to Vienna during the years when the library was being excavated. As the inscriptions on the bases indicate, the statues symbolized the wisdom (sophia), knowledge (episteme), intelligence (ennoia) and virtue (arete) of Celsus.

The columns of the upper storey are smaller than the lower ones and support the triangular and semicircular frontals. There is a window below each frontal.

78- The Celsus Library.

The interior of the library measures 10.92 by 16.72 metres and is covered with decorative marble. The section of the western wall above the tomb of Celsus is apsidal. It is agreed that the statue discovered during

the excavations belongs either to Celsus or to his son, and it must have been located in this semicircular niche. It is now exhibited in the İstanbul Archaeological Museum. On the side walls, there are rows of niches where the scrolls were kept. The same type of niche is seen in the upper sections of the walls, too. The remains indicate that the interior of the library was not two-storeyed, and that there was a balcony with railing in front of the niches, located where the second storey should have been.

To prevent humidity, areas behind the walls with niches were left empty. The niche on the right stretches up to the burial chamber of Celsus. There were twelve thousand scrolls kept in these niches. Since the builder of the edifice, Tiberius Julius Aquila, son of Celsus, died before the completion of the building, his heirs completed the construction. Tiberius Julius Aquila had bequeathed 25,000 dinars on the condition that scrolls would be acquired.

Since the library was built after the structures on each side of it, it was squeezed in between. Therefore, it was designed to look wider than it actually was. For example, the columns stand on a convex podium, the columns, capitals and the rafters on the side were made smaller than the ones in the centre, so that they would look as though they were situated farther from the others. Thus the structure looks wider than it actually is.

In 262, during the Gothic attacks, the interior of the library was burnt completely but the facade was not affected much. Towards the end of the 4th century it was repaired along with many other buildings in Ephesus, and the small fountain next to the steps in the front was erected. The facade collapsed during an earthquake around the 10th century (It was restored by F. Hueber).

In the course of excavations, blocks of a frieze depicting the Parthian wars were discovered standing in a row on both sides of the fountain in front of the library. According to one theory, the frieze belonged to an altar located on the south side of the square in front of the library. The steps of the road leading down to the library, together with the steps in front of the altar and the library itself, create an auditorium-like appearance.

The wall and the gate built with plaster and rubble seen in the centre of the square, were erected in the 6th-7th centuries when the population of Ephesus was sparse. They were the city walls and the gate in the west. The sarcophagus located on the side of the square was discovered in 1968 during the excavations organized by the Ephesus Museum. It had already been robbed. The inscription on it indicates that the sarcophages belonged to Tiberius Claudius Flavianus Dionysios and was made in the 2nd century.

30-31. THE MAZEUS-MITHRIDATES GATE AND THE AGORA (MARKET PLACE)

The gate located between the Agora and the Celsus library has three passages like a Roman triumphal arch. Wide and strong pilasters between the passages supports the arch and the frieze which is on top of the arch. The frieze consists of three sections and is richly decorated. The attic walls are found on top of the frieze. The passage in the middle was built recessed to give depth to the structure. Also, together with the walls of the attic, it makes the structure look "crowned". There are two apsidal niches in each side passage. "Whoever urinates here will be tried in court" is written in the second niche in the eastern passage. The main inscription of the gate is seen on the attics located above the side passages.

The inscription on the west states:

Im (peratori) Caesari Divi f(ilio) Augusto pontifici maximo co(n)s (uli) XII. tribunic (ia) potest (ate) XX et

Liviae   Caesaris   Augsti

Mazeus   et

The inscription on the east states:

M. Agrippae L(ucii) f(ilio) co(n)s (uli) tert(ium)

imb(eratori) tribunic(ia)

potest(ate)   VI   et

Iuliae   Caesaris   Augusti   fil(iae)

Mithridates   patronis

The inscription is in Latin. The bronze letters were mounted on the attics. In the second line of the inscription on the eastern attic, "imp" was spelled as "imb" by mistake. The inscription states verbatim: To the Emperor Caesar, Augustus, son of a god, the high priest, twelve times consul, twenty times tribune, and Livia, wife of Caesar Augustus, to Marc Agrippa, son of Lucius, three times consul, emperor, six times tribune and daughter of Julio Caesar Augustus, our patrons Mazeus and Mithridates (dedicate this arch).

Mazeus and Mithridates were slaves of Emperor Augustus and his family. When they were emancipated, after receiving permission from Emperor Augustus, they built this gate either in 4 or 3 B.C. and dedicated it to Augustus, his wife Livia, his daughter Julia and his son-in-law Agrippa.

The restoration of the gate is still going on. During excavations it was discovered that the wide drainage system from Curetes Street passed under this gate.

The Market Place (Agora)

Besides the Mazeus Mithridates Gate, the Agora has two other gates; one located in the west and the other in the north. The western gate has many columns and exhibits exquisite craftsmanship. The restoration of this gate and the northern gate, on which we have no information yet as to what they looked like, has not been started.

The Agora exhibits a square plan, each side measuring 111 metres. It was first built in the 3rd century B.C. and attained its final form during the reign of Emperor Caracalla (211-217). During excavations, the remains of the original Agora was seen 2-2.5 metres below the ground level today. Most of the Agora was destroyed by earthquakes in the 4th century, but it was rebuilt later.

In the north, outside the Agora, on all three sides, there were small storerooms with vaulted roofs. Those in the south and the east had two storeys. Right in front of the storerooms there are two rows of columns supporting a roof. Originally the columns were made of granite, but in the

79- The Agora and the
Stoa of Nero. 1st
century A.D..

80- The Commercial
Agora. 1st century
A.D..

course of restorations in the 4th century, marble columns were also used.

In the middle of the Agora which resembles a large square, there used to be a sundial and a water clock (a horologium). The remains of its foundation were seen during excavations.

In the vacant area in the middle of the Agora, the inscriptions of the statues of many philosophers, orators, state officials and scholars were discovered.

During the Roman period, the Agoras (forums) occupied an important place in the life of a city. Since these were considered semi-sacred areas, one entered agoras with reverence as though entering a place of worship. The famous Roman philosopher Cato once said, "One does not enter a forum wearing the same suit as is worn in the fields". In agoras, bronze and copper objects produced by using the latest technique of the day, various ceramic ware (especially oil lamps), herbs from Arabian countries, wine produced in Anatolia, honey and cured meat, as well as silk, perfume made in Ephesus, and jewellery made of precious stones were sold.

32. THE TEMPLE OF SERAPIS

The road with steps which passes by the south-western corner of the Agora leads to the Serapion, as well as the road which starts at the western gate of the Agora. This 24 metres wide and 160 metres long road which resembles a stoa, is paved with marble. It leads to a door reached by steps at the south side of the temple. The door opens onto a spacious courtyard which is enclosed on three sides by a columned portico. The Temple of Serapis is built on a terrace higher than the courtyard.

The prostyle (preceded by a porch with columns in the front) temple consists of a porch (pronaos) and the main chamber (naos). The columns of the pronaos measure 1.5 metres in diameter and have Corinthian capitals. It has been established that each column weighs 57 tons, and the other structural elements on the columns weigh about the same. The entrance of the temple is very wide and has two doors made of metal. The castors of the doors have left deep prints in the stylobate (the upper step of the temple).

The incomplete structural elements seen around the temple indicate that the temple was not completed. An Egyptian style statue made of granite was discovered during excavations. An inscription unearthed, mentions that the temple was dedicated to Serapis. The Roman religions did not believe in "life after death". According to them, as Homeros mentioned also, the spirits of the dead moved around in Hades and usually suffered pain, whereas the Egyptian religions promised incarnation and life in the other world.

Good relations between Egypt and Ephesus reached their peak during the Persian era. The trade realized by ships travelling directly between Ephesus and Alexandria is the most convincing proof of this. Many statues of Egyptian origin unearthed in the course of excavations in Ephesus, and a peace treaty displayed today in the Ephesus Museum, also prove the close relationship between Ephesus and Egypt. The marble peace treaty is 1 metre long, and on one side, Artemis, the most powerful goddess of

Ephesus, and on the other side, Serapis, the most important Egyptian god, holding a sceptre and wearing a beard, are depicted. Therefore, the cult of the god Serapis was observed in Ephesus, and in the 2nd century during the period of Antonius, this highly decorated temple was constructed and dedicated to him.

81- Aphrodite. Marble.
1st century A.D..

82- A statuette of Serapis. Bronze. 2nd. century A.D..

83- The Marble Road.

84- The Marble Road.

33. THE MARBLE ROAD

The sacred road which encircles Panayır Dağı is called Marble Road, and runs between the Celsus Library and the Theatre. It is paved with large and regular marble slabs. There is a columned portico along its eastern side, just like Curetes Street. Its western side was raised 2 metres and turned into a covered stoa during the reign of Emperor Nero (54-65). The entrance of the stoa is in the direction of the Theatre and has steps. Restoration of the stoa has not been completed yet. Originally, steel and lead clamps were used to hold the blocks of the wall together, but these were removed during the Byzantine era when Ephesus was economically quite weak. The holes seen in the walls today were made when these clamps were removed.

There is a narrow pavement on the side of the·street by the stoa. The figures of a woman's head, a left foot and supposedly a heart are seen on this pavement. These date back to the Byzantine era and were made to advertise the Brothel in a facetious manner. The reliefs of gladiators also found on this side of the street, were brought here from different locations in the city.

The Marble Road originates at Celsus Library, and passes through the Koressos Gate between the Vedius Gymnasium and the Stadium, and continues further. In the 5th century, an Ephesian named Eutropis repaired this section of the road, and in gratitude, the Ephesians erected his bust onthe street.

The sections of the road which were not repaired during antiquity, bear the impressions of the wheels of the Roman carriages. These impressions are 10 to 15 centimetres long.

The excavation and restoration of the road beyond the Theatre Gymnasium are being carried out by the Ephesus Museum. A well-preserved section of an arch made of regular bricks, indicates that there were arches made of brick between the columns, and that the porticos were roofed with wood. During restorations in the 4th century, rows of seats were brought here from the Stadium and used as parapets. Also, the granite columns were brought here from the Agora.

34. THE THEATRE

The Theatre built on the slopes of Panayır Dağı was constructed during the reign of Lysimachos, and later it was altered many times. Like all the other ancient theatres, the Theatre consisted of three main sections: the skene (stage building), the orchestra (place of action for the actors), and the cavea (auditorium) where the audience sat. The skene which was approximately 18 metres high, was the most imposing section of the Theatre. The facade of the structure which faced the audience was three-tiered and had columns. There were statues in the niches behind the columns, and the niches had either triangular or semicircular frontals. The well-preserved ground floor consists of an entrance which stretches in a north-south direc-

tion, and has eight rooms in a row, to the west of the entrance. The rooms at each end open onto a narrow terrace in the west of the building. A narrow door in the middle gave access to the orchestra.

During the Classical period (5th century B.C.), a separate stage building was not included in the plan of a theatre. Actors performed with the chorus in the orchestra. Sometimes, the area where actors performed was built slightly higher than the orchestra. During the Hellenistic period, the orchestra became smaller, and small and narrow stages began to be built for the performers. As a result, spectators sitting in the front could see better, and those sitting in the back could hear better. The stage of the Hellenistic theatre in Ephesus was 2.5-3 metres wide and as much in height. During the Roman Empire, both the width and the length of the stage were increased to 6 metres and 25.6 metres respectively. The distinguished citizens of Ephesus sat in the seats in the orchestra.

During the reign of Emperor Claudius (31-42), the Theatre was altered to meet the demands of the day. Although the stage building stayed the same, it was extended forward about 3 metres, towards the centre of the orchestra. Two rows of columns were used for the construction of this section called the proskene. These are seen even today. Also, an imposing facade displaying three tiers of columns, was built on the main building behind the proskene. This facade was decorated with niches, statues and reliefs. In the course of these additions, the paradoses (side entrances) on both sides of the orchestra were covered, and the tunnel-like entrances we see today were constructed. The one in the north is in a good state of preservation but the southern one was altered again. There are five doors which open onto the proskene from the main building. The door in the middle is the largest, and those at each end are the smallest. This gradual decrease in size toward the ends makes the building look larger. Either a bust or a statue of the Emperor must have been placed in the niche which would have been situated above the door in the middle.

These alterations which had started during the time of Emperor Claudius, were completed in seventy years. When St. Paul came to Ephesus, these alterations were still underway.

85- The Theatre.

86- Plan of the Theatre. Wilberg.

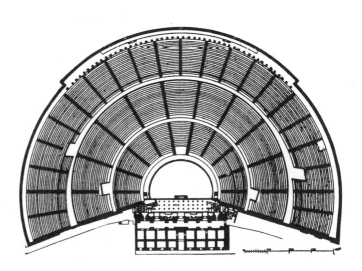

87- The Stage building (skcne) of the Theatre.

A section of the second storey of the stage building was discovered very well-preserved. As this section indicated, the floor plan of the second storey was different from the ground floor. In the middle, there was a long hallway with five doors on the side with the proskene, and there were two rows of rooms on its western side.

The Orchestra: The diameter of the orchestra which is slightly larger than a semicircle is 34 metres.

During plays, members of the chorus entered through the paradoses and took their places on each side of the orchestra. When it was their turn, they all talked simultaneously. Before the performances, a ceremony honouring Dionysus, took place in front of the altar which must have been in the centre of the orchestra. The origin of the plays performed, were the prayers and the ceremonies dedicated to the god of wine, Dionysus. This is why it was traditional to have a ceremony and sacrifice animals for Dionysus before the start of each performance.

The orchestra of the Hellenistic theatre was smaller. Today, only the remains of its canals can be seen. During the Roman Empire, the diameter of the orchestra was increased about 5 metres. Its floor was covered with marble slabs, some of which were green. The covering we see today, was made to match the few original marble slabs that are extant.

The cavea where the audience sat is also larger than a semicircle. The distance from the floor of the orchestra to its highest point measures almost 38 metres and its diameter is about 154 metres. It is wide enough to seat

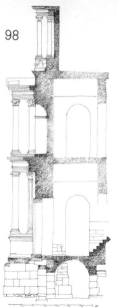

88- The Stage building of the Theatre.

24,000. The two diazomas (passages) divide the cavea into three sections, and there are twelve ascending stairways.

The spectators reached their seats through the staircases outside the cavea, and the entrance was from a road on top of the hill against which the theatre rested. A columned gallery above the highest row of seats both bordered this section of the theatre and improved the accoustics. Originally between the orchestra and the cavea, there was an iron railing, but later, the railing was replaced by a 2 metres high wall. The cavea, like the stage building, attained its final form after the alterations which took place during the reigns of Emperor Nero (54-68) and Emperor Septimus Severus (193-211).

All the performers were male and they wore masks during performances, as seen in the frescoes depicting scenes from plays, in the houses on the slopes. The spectators were very familiar with the stories of the plays which started early in the morning.

Meeting called "Demos" where all the Ephesians attended, were held in the Theatre of Ephesus.

35. THE HELLENISTIC FOUNTAIN

There is a small but exquisite fountain on the right, at the corner of the Theatre facing the street. It has two columns with Ionic capitals and a small pool. Water cascaded into the pool through the marble lion heads.

The fountain was erected in the 2nd century B.C. and it was widened in the 4th century by the addition of two ordinary looking columns.

36. THE HARBOUR STREET

The street that stretches between the Theatre and the harbour is called both Arcadiana and Harbour Street. Since Arcadius (395-408), son of the Eastern Roman Emperor Theodosius, remodelled and repaired the road and erected an inscription, the street is called Arcadiana.

Harbour Street is 500 metres long and 11 metres wide. On both sides of the street there were covered porticos, the floors of which were paved with mosaics, and behind these porticos, there were stores. The street was first built in the 1st century B.C. and it was truly a ceremonial road. The roads from Anatolia ended here. Many famous personalities who came from overseas, as well as emperors and proconsuls entered the city through this street.

One of the inscriptions unearthed during excavations states "On the columned porticos along both sides of Arcadiana, there are fifty lamps up to the statue of the boar". During antiquity, very few cities were lit. Among these we can name only Rome, Ephesus and Antioch. The boar mentioned in the text, refers to the boar in the story of the establishment of Ephesus by Androklos.

Only the foundations of the gates resembling triumphal archs, which were situated near the harbour and the Theatre, remain. In the 5th century, statues of the four Evangelists used to be on the four columns erected in the middle section of the street. The shafts of the columns are extant. The text of an inscription found in the street indicates the taxes paid for official business in Ephesus. According to the text, the tax paid to sell parsley was 1 denarius; to sell salt was 1 denarii; to be declared a champion in the games was 6 denarii; to obtain a birth certificate was 1 denarius but if the mother belonged to a distinguished class, then it was 100 denarius. It was worth paying that much money to obtain such a prestigious birth certificate.

89- The Harbour Street.

37. THE THEATRE GYMNASIUM

The biggest gymnasium in Ephesus is situated to the north of the square where Harbour street and Marble Road intersect each other. The excavation of only the palaestra (training school for physical exercises) of the gymnasium has been completed. The palaestra, built facing Harbour Street, measures 70 by 30 metres and is surrounded on three sides by a columned portico. On its fourth side, there are steps which were isude as viewing stands during the practice sessions of various sports. The entrance to the main building from the palaestra was located here also. The main building was built in an east-west direction, on a symmetrical floor plan. The baths, including the frigidarium, tepidarium, caldarium and the other sections, are located at the southern end, adjacent to the palaestra. The classrooms were located at the sides. The five rooms in the north served as the library and conference rooms, and the one in the middle with an apsidal wall was the Imperial Hall of the gymnasium.

38. THE VERULANUS SPORTS ARENA

All along the northern side of Harbour Street there are sports establishments, the largest one of which is the Verulanus Sports Arena. It measures 200 by 240 metres and extends from the Theatre Gymnasium to the Harbour Gymnasium.

A beautiful gate with five passages, and a small street connects the Verulanus Sports Arena to Harbour Street. The Arena consists of a ring in the centre and a marble paved portico surrounded by three rows of columns. It is connected to the Gymnasium located to the west of it and was built during the reign of Emperor Hadrian (117-138) by the high priest of the Asian province.

39. THE HARBOUR GYMNASIUM AND ITS PALAESTRA

The Gymnasium is located to the west of the Verulanus Sports Arena and there is a wide passage between them. The main entrance is through an elliptical courtyard, which is paved with mosaics and surrounded by columns. To the north of this entrance there is a door which opens onto the Atrium. On each side of the door there is a pool decorated with bulls' heads carrying garlands.

The building measures 40 by 20 metres and has a palaestra paved with coloured marble. The palaestra is surrounded by rooms (as in other gymnasiums) that were used by the students for various purposes. The Imperial Hall is located in the north and its northern wall is apsidal.

The bronze statue of an athlete, the marble statue of a boy playing with a duck, the statue of Heracles-Kentauros discovered in the course of excavations of the two-storeys high gymnasium were taken to Vienna. The Harbour Gymnasium was built during the reign of Emperor Hadrian.

40. THE HARBOUR BATHS

This is built in a north-south direction between the harbour and the Gymnasium. The Harbour Baths are one of the largest edifices in Ephesus and measure 160 by 170 metres, standing 28 metres high. To the east of the structure there is a long hall which extends the length of the structure. The frigidarium is in the middle of this hall and the dressing rooms are located on both sides of it. A large elliptical pool measuring 30 metres in length, is located in the centre of the frigidarium. A row of 11 metres high columns made of pink and gray granite and their marble composite capitals, support the vaulted roof made of brick. In the dressing areas, there are thick pillars made of large blocks of stones with wide niches between them.

Many statues were unearthed during the excavation of these sections and the bases of the statues can be seen today. The caldarium, which was the warmest section of the baths, is located to the west of the frigidarium, and it resembles a large hall with a high ceiling. It is entered either directly from the frigidarium or through the other sections located on each side.

The Harbour Baths were built in the 2nd century and renovated during the reign of Constantine II (337-361).

THE HARBOUR

A magnificent gate at the end of Harbour Street opens onto the harbour of Ephesus.

90- The Harbour Baths. 2nd century.

The alluvium deposited by the Küçük Menderes (Kaystros) river throughout the centuries finally deprived Ephesus of its harbour. Although the swampy area has not been excavated yet, the remains of structures like warehouses are seen in the vicinity. There is also a small lake, the last remnant of the harbour.

The location of Ephesus on a busy sea traffic lane was the most important factor contributing to its development. Hence, throughout its history, it had been necessary to take precautions against the deposit of alluvium. Although Attalos II, the King of Pergamum, had wanted to deepen the opening of the harbour and had built a retaining wall enabling large ships to come closer to the shore, it was never used since the harbour filled up very fast.

In 61, the proconsul of the time tried to deepen the harbour, and in the next century when Emperor Hadrian came to Ephesus, he tried to move the bed of Kaystros which drained into the harbour. An inscription states that an Ephesian spent 20,000 denarii to clean the harbour. Yet, all these efforts failed and the harbour filled up. Today, only a small lake in a swampy area 4.5 km. inland is all that is left of it.

41. THE CHURCH OF THE VIRGIN MARY (THE COUNCIL CHURCH)

91- Apse of the Church of the Virgin Mary (the Council Church) after restorations.

This is located to the north of the Harbour Baths. The main entrance of the church is on the side facing Kuşadası. The church has an important place in the history of Christianity, since it is the first church ever dedicated to the Virgin Mary. Also, it is the place where the Ecumenical Council met in 431 to discuss the principles of Christianity. The 260 metres long and 30 metres wide edifice was built in the 2nd century as a museion, which was a school for higher education. Medicine and other sciences were taught and discussions were held here. Also, the priests who had important duties in Ephesus completed their training in the museion. An inscription found in the area mentions that the physicians and the professors who served at the Ephesus Museion were exempt from tax. This applied not only within the borders of the Asian province but in all the precincts within the province. It was a real burden to pay custom duties while travelling in the province, although it seemed unimportant. Exempting the physicians and the professors from this burden indicates the importance given to the Museion.

The Museion which had three naves and a basilical plan, was converted into a basilica in the 4th century. In the course of alterations, an apse was built in the eastern wall, an atrium surrounded by columns was built in the west, and the baptistry was constructed to the north of the atrium. The nave in the middle is as wide as the apse and the side naves are smaller. Between the naves, there are columns and plaques decorated with geometric designs. The narthex is located at the western end of the edifice. It is a narrow hall, the floor or which is paved with mosaics of geometric designs. The floor of the atrium is covered with large slabs brought here from different places in Ephesus. Some of these are decorated and some have inscriptions on them. The western wall is apsidal. The baptistry is circular and the baptismal pool is located in the centre. There are six niches in the walls, which supported a domed roof. Around this main hall there is a hallway, and on the western side there are three small rooms which belonged to the priests who performed baptisms.

During the reign of Emperor Justinian (527-565) the basilica was altered again. A small church with a dome was constructed between the apse and the narthex. A small vaulted room was built on each side of the apse, and doors with wide arches were built in the north and the south, giving access to the church. The exonarthex built in front of the narthex in the west, completed the church. The marble cauldron (omphalos) seen today in the centre of the church, was brought from the Harbour Baths and used in the church. In the 10th century, the eastern section of the church was converted into another church and a small chapel was built at the southern end.

The restoration of the churc was started in 1984 by the Ephesus Museum. During the meeting of the Ecumenical Council in 431, the members discussed the thesis that the Virgin Mary was not the mother of Jesus, the son of God but the mother of Jesus, a mortal. Nestorius, the patriarch of Constantinople first proposed this thesis when he was in Antioch, and later defended it fervently in Constantinople. To prove his views he said that none of the disciples had said anything contrary to them. When the thesis created a turmoil, Emperor Theodosius ordered the third meeting of the Ecumenical Council in Ephesus. Nestorius, the patriarch of Constantinople; Cyril, the patriarch of Alexandria; John, the patriarch of Antiocheia; the patriarch of Ephesus and the representative of the Pope attended the meeting. These were uneasy days in Ephesus. Almost two hundred religious authorities discussed the issue for three months. They also recorded in the proceedings of this meeting that when the Virgin Mary came to Ephesus, he stayed in the house which had been located at the site of this church and that she was buried in Ephesus.

42. THE BYZANTINE BATHS

In the middle of the square at the north exit of Ephesus, there are the remains of a structure indicating a complex floor plan. It belongs to the baths built in the 6th century. A large hall with an apse at each end stretches along the western side of the building. It can be called a "rest area". On the side facing the street in the east, it has two structural complexes that look separated and different from each other. In the middle of the one in the south, there is a hall with curved corners. The function of this hall has not yet been established. The doors in the east and west give access to smaller halls with an apse. The other side of the structure exhibits a more complex plan. The tepidarium is in the middle and there are many small rooms on the eastern side. Many large earthenware jars were unearthed during the excavations.

43. THE ACROPOLIS

The small hill to the north of the Byzantine Baths is assumed to be the Acropolis. The most recent excavations revealed that a fortification wall surrounded the hill. Since these walls were built before the city walls constructed during the reign of Lysimachos, the hill, most probably, was the early acropolis. Preliminary excavations carried on at the northern and western sides of the hill did not reveal any remains. Therefore, it has been concluded that in ancient times these areas were under the sea. We can also safely assume that the original harbour of Ephesus, Koressos Harbour, was located here.

The foundation of a multi-cornered structure was discovered on the Acropolis. The structure dated to the 6th or 7th century B.C. and was the oldest building in Ephesus. We still do not know why it was built. It is assumed that this is the location where the founder of Ephesus, Androklos, son of Kodros, after killing the boar, built a temple and dedicated it to Apollo in gratitude.

THE FOUNTAIN

There is an appealing fountain with three niches on the side of Acropolis Hill facing Ephesus. There is a pool in front of each niche, and some of these pools are decorated with signs of the Cross. The fountain was constructed in the 6th century.

THE STADIUM

Located to the east of the Acropolis, at the foot of Panayır Dağı, the Stadium, measuring 230 metres long and 30 metres wide, is shaped like a horseshoe.

The Stadium had an important place in the lives of Ephesians since antiquity, various sports competitions like boxing, and wrestling etc... were held in the Stadium.

The entrance of the Stadium is located in the west. The gate at the entrance with its double row of columns, resembled a triumphal arch. The vase and the plaques, decorated with rabbit motifs, and seen in front of the entrance facing the street, were brought here from another location. The seats located at the foot of the hill were carved out of natural rock in the form of steps. The other side was raised with vaulted galleries and the seats were placed on them. These vaulted galleries resemble long rooms and every seven to eight metres there are small holes which open into the rooms.

The Stadium was built during the Hellenistic era, and during the reign of Nero (54-68) it was restored to its present condition. In the 3rd and the 4th centuries, the arched entrances to the west of the seats were altered.

During the 3rd and 4th centuries, gladiators and wild animal fights were quite popular in the Roman world. These games were held in the stadiums and theatres in front of a large audience. Christians were murdered during these wild animal fights. This is why, after Christianity became the official religion, the Ephesus Stadium was destroyed unmercifully by religious fanatics, as though to take revenge.

Therefore today, there is not even one well-preserved row of seats to be found in the Stadium. Some of the exquisitely crafted rows of seats with inscriptions on them were used in the construction and restoration of other buildings during the 4th and the 6th centuries.

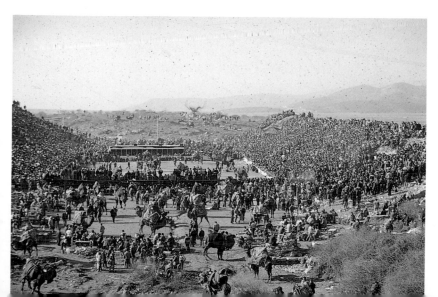

92 Ephesus Stadium, traditional camel fight, January 1989.

45. THE VEDIUS GYMNASIUM

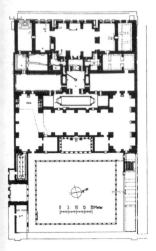

93- The Vedius
Gymnasium. M.
Theuer.

This large edifice is located to the north of the Stadium, and according to an inscription, it was built by P. Vedius Antonius and his wife Flavia Papiana. The Vedius family was one of the most well-known families in Ephesus. The edifice was dedicated to Artemis and their close friend Emperor Antonius Pius (138-161).

The Vedius Gymnasium is one of the most beautiful structures in Ephesus. It has many rooms, and the entrance located in the east resembles a monumental propylon (the entrance building of a sacred area). A statue of the emperor used to be in the niche seen in the western wall of the propylon with columns. A group of structures is found to the west of the propylon. The palaestra which measures 40 by 50 metres and has a portico surrounded by 5 metres high columns, is located to the east of the propylon. The well-preserved latrina is by the columned door which opens onto the street south of the palaestra, and it does not have a roof. Only one door served both as the entrance and the exit of the latrina.

The first hall behind the propylon measures 20 by 10 metres, and it was either an imperial hall or a ceremonial hall. After this hall comes the frigidarium with a large pool, and the other rooms which are situated symmetrically in an east-west direction.

Almost half of the edifice has been excavated, and the statues unearthed have been taken to the İzmir Archaeological Museum.

The excavation of the substructure of the Gymnasium which seems to have arches and halls, has not been started yet.

46. THE CAVE OF THE SEVEN SLEEPERS

The asphalt road that turns east by the Vedius Gymnasium, leads to the Cave of the Seven Sleepers.

The Christians in the early empire, were in a dispute with the Roman state over the subject of the imperial cult, according to which, those Christians who refused to sacrifice animals at an imperial temple, were considered enemies of the state, and they were treated as such. The story of the Seven Sleepers is based on this dispute.

Around 250, during the reign of Emperor Decius, seven Christian young men escaped from the city and took refuge in a cave, since they had refused to sacrifice animals at the imperial temple. After a while these seven young men fell asleep, and when they woke up they went to the city to buy food. To their amazement, they found out that they had slept not for one night but for two hundred years, and that Christianity had spread to every corner of the Roman Empire. When Emperor Theodosius II heard the incident, he accepted it as evidence of resurrection which was being discussed in the churches then.

When these young men died, following an impressive funeral, they were buried in the cave on which a church was built later. The excavations carried on here during 1927-1928 brought to light a church, and several

94- Head of Zeus.
Marble. 1st century.

95- Head of a Goddess.
Marble. 2nd century.

hundred graves which were dated to the 5th and 6th centuries. Inscriptions dedicated to the Seven Sleepers were found on the walls of the church and in the graves.

For hundreds of years, people wanted to be buried as close as possible to the Seven Sleepers who were considered holy. According to a Christian belief, St. Mary Magdalene is buried here, also.

47. THE CHURCH OF ST. JOHN

This most magnificient Byzantine edifice in Ephesus is located at the southern foot of the hill where the Selçuk Castle is situated. The historian Eusibios stated that between 37 and 42, the apostles who were trying to spread Christianity were expelled from Jerusalem, and that St. John came to Anatolia and continued his sacred mission. Therefore we know that St. John was in Ephesus during those years, with the Virgin Mary who was entrusted to him by Jesus.

Following the assassination of St. Paul, St. John assumed the authority of all the churches under the Church of Ephesus and wrote his gospel. According to his will, St. John was buried here, in the church which bears his name. In the 4th century, when Christianity had started gaining strength in Ephesus, a basilica with a wooden roof was built over his grave, and during the reign of the Byzantine Emperor Justinian (527-565), a church, the remains of which we can see today, was built. In the 7th and 8th centuries when Ephesus was attacked by the Arabs, a fortification wall was

96- The Church of St. John.

built around the church, and by connecting the area to the fortress on top of the hill, the church was turned into an outpost.

According to written sources, in the beginning of the Middle Ages the church was in great need of repairs, but since it was believed that the dust in the burial chamber had healing powers, the church was visited by invalids who came from far away lands, and the church continued to be one of the most important shrines for Christians.

Ibni Batuta, the traveller, stated that, in the 14th century during the Dynasty of Aydınoğulları, it served as a mosque. The foundation of its minarets seen at the entrance to the narthex belong to this period.

In the 14th century following the construction of the famous İsa Bey Mosque, the church lost its importance and at the end of the same century, it collapsed in an earthquake.

The archaeologist Sotiriu started excavating the church between 1921 and 1922. Later, a large section of it was unearthed by the Austrian Archaeological Institute. Between 1957 and 1958, it was restored, and the columns of the second storey that were discovered in the northern nave, were erected. In 1960, the Ephesus Museum started excavating and restoring the church. Since 1973, under the direction of Prof. E. Akurgal, the Ephesus Museum has been steadily excavating and restoring the church. These last projects are being financed by the Office of Ancient Treasures and Museums of the Ministry of Culture and Tourism, and the Quadman Foundation of the United States.

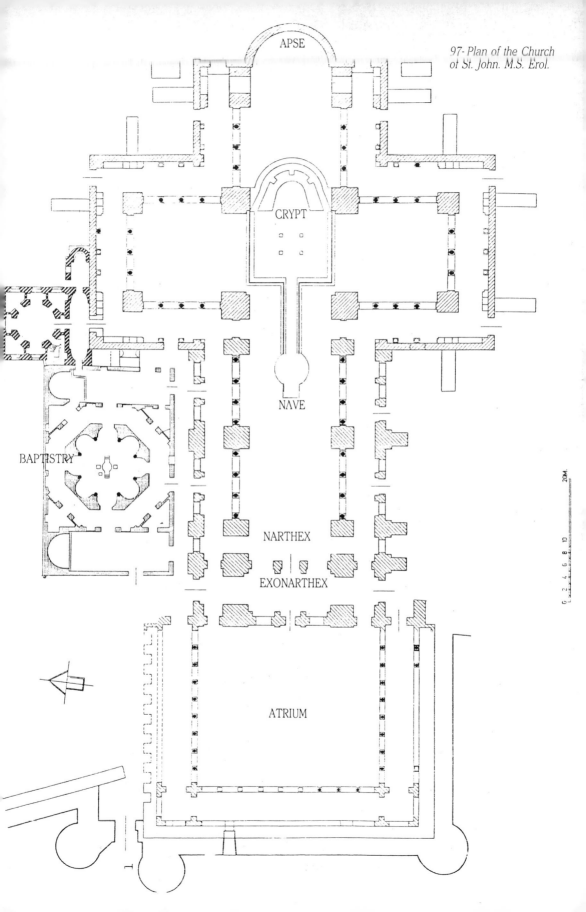

APSE

97- Plan of the Church
of St. John. M.S. Erol.

CRYPT

NAVE

BAPTISTRY

NARTHEX

EXONARTHEX

ATRIUM

20 M.

0 2 4 6 8 10

98- The Church of St. John. H. Hormann - C. Koççoban.

The Pursuit Gate and the Fortification Walls

The fortification wall which surrounds the church has three gates and twenty towers, each with a different floor plan. The most impressive gate is the Pursuit Gate located facing the parking lot. The other two gates are in the east and west. The Western Gate is in the direction of Ephesus and has two round towers and a small courtyard. The road with steps which winds up from İsa Bey Mosque at the foot of the hill reaches this gate. The gate and its courtyard have been restored. The excavation of the Eastern Gate has not been completed yet.

The marble used in the construction of the towers and the fortification walls was brought from Ephesus, particularly from the Stadium. In the 3rd and 4th centuries, when gladiators and wild animal fights became very popular, the eastern end of the Stadium was converted into an arena where Christians were tortured. This is why the Stadium was destroyed with such vengeance, and its construction materials were used in building the church and the fortress.

The main entrance of the church is through the Pursuit Gate. The inclined marble road from the parking lot, leads to the gate, which has two monumental towers and an arched entrance. The frieze which used to be on the wall between the towers was about Achilles, and it has been taken to the Woburn Abbey Gallery in England. The entrance leads into a small courtyard. Since the gates were the weakest points of a fortress, the enemy usually attacked there. If the gates gave in under the attacks, then the enemy was let into the courtyard, the other side of which did not have an exit, and the enemy was defeated by attacks from the top of the courtyard walls. The Pursuit Gate is the last example of the gates with courtyards, which were built quite often in the Hellenistic period in Anatolia. The Roman inscriptions seen in the courtyard were discovered in the course of excavation of the church.

The Atrium

Located at the western end of the church, the Atrium measures 34 by

99- Restoration of the Church of St. John.

→

100- The Pursuit Gate. 6th century.

47 metres. In order to build it at the same level as the naves, the slope of the hill was eliminated by the construction of walls. There is an empty area in the centre surrounded by a columned portico, and outside there is an area with a railing for strolling. No traces of its floor covering have been discovered during excavations. The large earthenware jars seen in the centre belong to various periods. The cistern with three sections built under the western portico was enclosed by an arch.

The Narthex

The long and narrow narthex is located between the atrium and the naves. Three doors lead into the atrium and three other doors lead into the naves. The lintels of these doors are made of large blocks of marble. In modern times, a wall and doors were built between the atrium and the narthex, thus creating an exonarthex. The narthex used to have five small domes.

The Naves and the Burial Chamber

This is the main section of the church. With its cross-shaped plan and three naves it is a typical classical church. It had six large domes: two over the central nave, two at the transepts and two in between these. The side naves were vaulted.

The domes were supported by the marble and brick pillars that are still extant. Between the pillars, there are blue veined marble columns separating the naves. On the sides of the capitals facing the central nave, there are the monograms of Emperor Justinian and his wife Theodora. These monograms are definite proof of the age of the structure. The columns between the naves are connected to each other by arches which also support the upper row of columns. Traces of frescoes and mosaics are seen on the fragments of the dome discovered in the course of excavations.

The burial chamber is situated at the end of the central nave, in front of the apse. It was raised by two steps to make it more prominent. The coloured marble mosaics on it are reproductions faithful to the original. Its small dome supported by columns with spiral grooves, and the Iconastasis have collapsed completely. This section of the church and its ambon, connected to the church by a short path, are being restored.

The Chapel and the Treasury (Skeuophylakion)

The chapel is located on the side of the northern transept and it is temporarily covered by a wooden roof. It was originally a part of the Treasury section in the back, but in the 10th century it was converted into a chapel. Frescoes depicting St. John, Jesus and a saint, are seen in the apse. The entrance to the Treasury section is in front of this. A round room 6.3 metres in diameter in the middle, a hallway with an apsidal vault on each side and the chapel, form a complex. The interior divisions of the main structure in the centre was built so that it seems to have a cross-shaped plan. The rooms which make up the arms of the cross have collapsed completely.

Baptistry

The door of the narrow hallway in front of the Treasury section leads to the group of structures which make up the Baptistry. A long hallway which stretches along the northern nave connects the Baptistry to the church. A tomb which resembles a fountain with columns, and a frontal is seen in the hallway. It was built in the 6th century and later it was used as a fountain.

*102- Western walls of
the Church of St. John.*

*103- Western walls of
the Church of St. John.*

The Baptistry has a complex plan which consists of an octagonal baptismal hall in the centre, a narrow hallway, and a hall with an apse on each side of the baptismal hall, the floor of which is covered with marble. There is a circular baptismal pool with steps on two sides in the centre of the hall. The pool has columns and arches. The fragments found during excavations indicate that the dome was covered with glass mosaic.

The Baptistry was constructed in the 5th century, before the church was built, during the reign of Emperor Justinian.

THE HOUSE OF THE VIRGIN MARY

104- The House of the Virgin Mary.

According to St. John's Gospel, before His death, Jesus pointed at St. John and said, "Woman, here is your son" and then pointed at the Virgin Mary and said "Here is your mother". The minutes of the Ecumenical Council of 431 indicate that four or six years after the death of Jesus, St. John and the Virgin Mary came together to Ephesus, and for a short time stayed

in the building, a section of which is now under the Church of the Virgin Mary today. Later, St. John moved the Virgin Mary to a house he had prepared for her on Bulbul Dağı. As time went by, the location of the house where Mary spent the last days of her life was forgotten and it fell into ruins. Yet, shortly after the Middle Ages, the location of the house was often discussed again but no conclusion could be reached.

In 1878, Clément Brentano published the relevations of a German nun named Catherine Emmerich in "The Life of the Virgin Mary" written in French. The work brought new interest to the subject of the location of the Virgin Mary's house. In 1891, Eugene Poulin, a Lazarist priest who was the president of İzmir College, in order to check the validity of this devoted nun's revelations, entrusted a group under the leadership of a priest named Yung, with the search of the house. The group searched for a long time on the mountains south of Ephesus, and finaly found the house on Panayır Dağı, known as the House of the Virgin Mary.

Catherine Emmerich (1774-1824) had never left the town where she was born, yet her description of the house of Mary exactly fits the house at Panaya Kapulu. In order to indroduce the house to the world, Eugéne Poulin published a series of articles and succeeded in getting a lot of attention. Most of the religious experts who visited the house accepted it as the house of the Virgin Mary. The patriarch of İzmir, Monseigneur Timoni, after serious research, gave permission in 1892 to conduct religious ceremonies here. In 1961, Pope John XXIII put an end to the dispute still going on over the location of the house of the Virgin Mary, by announcing it a place of pilgramage. In 1967, Pope Paul VI and in 1979 Pope John Paul II visited the house, and therefore indicated the importance they placed on the house.

The road which stretches from the Magnesia Gate toward Bülbül Dağı reaches the house. The remains of a round cistern in the small square located 100 metres from the house, and its arched wall on the side facing the hill, were discovered first. The steps on the side of the cistern are completely destroyed, only a section which resembles a pool is extant. In the course of excavations carried on near the wall, two sarcophagi made of baked clay were discovered. Each contained a skeleton, the skull of which was turned toward the house and burial gifts. One of the two coins found in the sarcophagi belonged to the reign of Emperor Constantine and the other to the reign of Emperor Justinian.

There is a small, domed church with a cross-shaped plan at the end of the road that leads from the cistern. This building is known as the House of the Virgin Mary and it dates to the 6th-7th centuries.

When it was discovered, only its foundation and parts of its walls were standing. It has been restored to its present state. In order to indicate the original walls, a red line was drawn between these and the new walls. An entrance with door-like niches on both sides, leads into a vaulted vestibule whence one enters the hall with an apse. The statue of the Virgin Mary found in the apse, had been placed there about one hundred years ago. Since the grey area in front of the apse is different from the rest of the marble paved floor, it must have been the location of the hearth. The pieces of coal found during excavations and a section of the foundation were dated to the first century. The small room in the south is known as the bedroom and there is an apsidal niche in its eastern wall. Since the Virgin Mary is also revered by Muslims, they pray (perform namaz) in this room. Inscriptions seen on the walls are interpretations of the section of the Koran relating to the Virgin Mary. Also, for those who want further information, there are many Korans in different languages in a special chest. The remains of another room which should be located symmetrically to this one have not been discovered yet. On the second terrace to the west of the house, there are fountains, the waters of which supposedly have medicinal qualities. The water supply of these fountains comes from under the pink coloured marble floor covering of the bedroom.

EPHESUS
MUSEUM

105- The Hall of the Residential Relics.

THE HALL OF THE RESIDENTIAL RELICS

During the last thirty years of excavations in the center of Roman Ephesus some of the houses of the distinguished citizens of Ephesus were also excavated. These houses, situated on the terraces that start from the southern side of the Curetes Street and expand towards the slopes of Bülbül Mountain are referred to as the "Houses or Palaces on the Slopes". They were built on a peristyle plan which was the most popular and widely used house plan in Roman times. The main feature of this type of houses was the small courtyard surrounded by rooms of different sizes. Almost all of these rooms were decorated with frescoes and mosaics. Excavations showed that the oldest peristyle house had been built in the 1st century A.D. and they were continued to be built until the 7th century. They were destroyed many times by earthquakes and fires but were restored each time. Due to the circumstances of the times, and the bad economic situation the Roman Empire was in, each time less attention was paid to the decorative elements and the construction material used in the restorations.

During the excavations, mostly household items and statuettes were discovered. Among the household items, there were bronze and marble tables, pitchers, stools, amphoras and kitchen bowls. The statuettes belong to gods, goddesses, emperors and priests. Few decorative objects and toys

106 - *An Egyptian priest, bronze, 6th century B.C.*

107 - *Head of Socrates, marble, 1st century.*

were also found. Until 1978, all the artifacts discovered, including the frescoes and the mosaics, used to be brought to the museum to be displayed but since then, the findings have been exhibited in situ. All of the relics seen in the first hall of the museum, the Hall of the Residential Relics, were unearthed during the excavation of the houses. Copies of some of them are displayed in the restored houses.

In the first showcase seen on the left upon entrance into the hall, the bronze treasures are displayed. The large Oinoche (pitcher) is dated to the 5th century B.C. and it was used as a wine container during the feasts. The reliefs around the mouth and below the handle were the main elements used in dating it. In 1972, it was stolen and smuggled to Switzerland from where it was taken to the Metropolitan Museum of Art to be put on exhibit, but upon recognition it was returned.

The statuette of a sitting, bearded man holding a spear belongs to Serapis, the principal god of Alexandria. In the Early Ages there was heavy

108 - *An oinoche (wine bowl), bronze, 5th century B.C.*

109 - *A statuette of İsis, bronze, 2nd century A.D..*

110 - Priapos, marble, 2nd century.

111 - Bronze snake, 1st century A.D.

trading between Ephesus and Alexandria and therefore many treasures were brought to Ephesus from Egypt. This statuette of Serapis was created in the 2nd century A.D.. The bronze statuette with the legs missing below the knees, displayed in the same showcase, belongs to Athena, the head goddess of Athens. She is described as a soldier wearing a helmet and an armour. The statuette was made in the 1st century A.D..

The marble statue of Ascleipus, next to the showcase, exhibits quality workmanship. The head and the caduceus (the symbol of the medical pro-

112 - Artemis the Archer, marble. 1st century.

113 - Bust of Livia, the wife of Emperor Augustus, marble, 1st century A.D.

fession) he is holding are missing. The most important centers of Asclepius are Pergamun and Epidaurus. For centuries the hospitals there were filled with patients seeking help. This statue of Ascleipus, which was made in the 1st century A.D., is the only statue discovered in Ephesus.

In the corner next to the statue of Asclepius are the busts of Emperor Tiberius and his mother, Livia. These were discovered with a bronze snake between them and they are being displayed the way they were found. The busts are in excellent condition. Tibcrius was the son of Emperor Augustus, and Livia was the wife of Augustus. The snake symbolizes the protector of the house. Its head was broken off in the first century by an unknown reason. It is described coiled and upright, ready to strike. It has scales and traces of gold plating. The busts, together with the snake, were made in the middle of the 1st century.

The rectangular marble block next to this is a commemorative inscription. On its front surface there are six garlands in three rows. In ancient

114 - Statue of Asclepius, marble, 1st century A.D.

times similar garlands used to be given as prizes in races. Every city had a sacred tree the leaves of which were used to make garlands.

The colossal head next to the commemorative block belongs to the goddess Athena. She is described looking straight ahead. On her forehead is the band of her helmet. Her hair is seen in thick curles hanging down to her neck from under her helmet. The holes in the forehead and the earlobes indicate that originally there were pieces of jewelry on the statue.

In the large showcase next to the head of Athena the small objects are displayed. The eye-catching, white marble, basket-shaped jewelry box is of high quality. On its opposite sides there are fruit and leafshaped handles. The lamps in the showcase indicate that many different shape lamps were used in the houses. One of the lamps is shaped like a foot wearing a sandal and the other one like an elephant. The other classic shaped lamps bear figures. On the base of the double lamp, there is the figure of Serapis,

115- Basket-shaped jewelry box, marble, 2nd century A.D.

the Egyptian god. Of the ivory objects in the showcase, the one shaped like Aphrodite, according a theory, was an ornamentation on a hairpin. The ones shaped like animal heads were knife handles. The others were pins and spoons used to prepare medicine. The earthenware statuettes, such as the small rooster, etc., displayed in the same showcase were made as children's toys. One of them has wheels so it could be pulled by a string. The flute is made of eagle's wings. The keys on it are similar to the ones on today's flutes. The colored glass bracelets in the showcase were very popular in the late Roman period. The bracelets made of precious metals like gold and silver were used by adults and those made of glass by children.

One of the most beautiful objects displayed in the hall is the "Eros on a Dolphin" statue displayed in the middle showcase. This bronze statuette served as the decorative element and the faucet of a fountain. Eros is depicted riding on a swimming dolphin and his hand is raised to express his pleasure. Water drained into the pool through the eyes of the dolphin.

The statuette was made in the 2nd century A.D.. Similar statuettes made of marble were quite popular and produced in abundance in Ephesus.

The first treasure in the showcase to the right of the entrance is the statue of Artemis. Since it is very similar to the statues made in the Archaic period, it is called the Archaic Artemis. It was made in the 2nd century A.D.. Originally, she was carrying an arrow in one hand and a bow in the other but they were broken off and are missing today. These and the traces of restoration seen on her right wrist indicate that it was damaged in the Roman era due to an unknown reason.

In the next showcase, a plate, one of the unique glass treasures in the museum, is displayed. One of the most beautiful examples of Roman art of glassworks, this plate was used as a fruit bowl. It was discovered in fragments and its missing parts have been replaced by polyester of the same color. The plate belongs to the 2nd century A.D.

116 - Eros on a Dolphin, bronze, 2nd century.

117 - Eros with a Rabbit, marble, 2nd century A.D..

118 - Comedy writer Menander's bust, 1st century A.D. copy.

120 · Bust of Attis, marble, 2nd century A.D.

119 · Childrens' bracelets, glass, 3-4 centuries A.D.

121 - Priapos, 2nd century.

One of the bronze portable tables used extensively in the houses in Ephesus is displayed in the showcase in the same row. The table has three legs and can be extended and raised as well. At the junction of the legs and the table top, there are decorations of boxers emerging through leaves. The sphere seen in the same showcase was the attribute of one of the distinguished citizens of Ephesus. The sphere, which used to be attached onto a long and thin pole through the hole in its lower section, consists of who circles surrounded by decorations of various motifs. It is assumed that it was made in the 1st century.

The statuette and statue of Pariapus located by the eastern wall of the hall are two of the unique treasures in the museum. Pariapus is god of nature and symbolizes nutritional fertility. The statue is made of marble and in the bowl placed on his phallus are the different kinds of fruit grown in Ionia.

These were considered essential for good health. He is wearing a shawl that does not cover the front part of his body. The face and the body of the earthenware Pariapus statuette in the showcase are caricaturized as his long phallus. In Egyptian mythology, this figure is known as God Bes and he is the protector of newborn male children and sleep. It used to be hung by a rope going through the now broken loop on its head.

The brown marble bust of Attis, one of the priests of Cybele, is on display in the large showcase in the same row. The left side of the bust and the front of the Frigian cap he is wearing are broken off and missing. The bust demonstrates high quality workmanship and it was made in the 2nd century A.D..

Of the other busts in the same showcase, the small one belongs to Gaius Caesar who was the son of Augustus' daughter, Agrippa. Caesar is depicted with childlike expression, and the bust demonstrates the distinct features of the age of Emperor Augustus.

The small bust the trunk of which is made of yellow-spotted onyx and the head of white marble belongs to an emperor and was made in the 2nd century A.D. In the Early Ages, many such statues, the heads of which were custom made separately, and busts were made. It was much easier and cheaper, upon the death or dethroning of an emperor, just to replace the head. The brown-spotted marble bust, which, apparently, was done with great care, most probably belonged to a prince. He is wearing a toga kept in place by a round pin on his right shoulder. The bust was made in the 2nd century A.D..

The white marble bust of Dionysus, the god of wine, is displayed in the same showcase. He is wearing a head band made of vine. The bust was created in the 2nd century A.D..

The small, black bust seen in the showcase is made of ivory. It was blackened due to a fire in one of the houses. It exhibits a distinct portrait style. Underneath the neck, there is a hole which was used to fasten it onto the trunk of a statue.

122 - Table leg depicting Dionysus, marble, 1st century A.D.

A marble statuette, also blackened by fire, is on exhibit in the same showcase. It describes a civil servant sitting in an ornate chair and holding a scroll. He looks typical of the classic civil servants of the time. The statuettes made of black or dark green Egyptian stones belong to the Egyptian gods and goddesses, and they were brought to Ephesus from Egypt during the period of heavy trade relations between Egypt and Ephesus. Almost all of these belong to the 6th and 7th centuries B.C..

One of the most valuable objects in this hall is the bronze statuette of an Egyptian priest. It is typical of classic Egyptian statuettes and the priest is described with his foot placed forward and his arms attached to his body. He is wearing a panther's skin with hieroglyphs on the back. He is wearing his attribute, a necklace with a cow head, around his neck. The statuette was brought from Egypt during trade relations between Ephesus and Egypt, particularly Alexandria. It was made in the 6th century A.D..

In the showcase by the eastern wall of the hall, the small objects are displayed. The most important one is the figure of a young maiden wearing a thin dress. It is situated in the middle of the showcase. The expression on her face is ideal. She is wearing a peplos. The figurine belongs to the 5th century. The other small figurines in the showcase were made between the 1st and the 3rd centuries. A.D.. The bronze bust of a philosopher, situated next to this showcase, exhibits intricate detail. He closely resembles the people in Anatolia today. The bust was made in 235-240 A.D.. The inclined, marble statuette exhibited in this showcase describes Marnas, the god of Manas Stream from which water was brought to Ephesus by aquaducts to the southeast. From the amphora under the arm of the semireclining Marnas ran the waters of Marnas Stream. The statuette was used as the faucet and decorative element of a fountain.

123 · Socrates Fresco, 2nd century.

In the showcases in the middle row, besides the statue of an Egyptian priest, the marble head of Eros, one of the unique treasures in the museum, is also on display. It is a Roman copy of the famous statue by the famous sculptor Lysippus. Eros in depicted using his bow, and with a childlike expression. It is one of the most significant works of sculpting.

The first statue displayed on the statue bases located by the wall behind the head of Eros is called "Eros with a Rabbit". Winged Eros is holding a rabbit and trying to rescue it from his dog described stretching towards the rabbit. Only the feet of the dog are extant. The other parts of its body have not been discovered. The statue was made in the 2nd century A.D..

The portrait of the slim-faced, older man, seen in the same row, belongs to the comedy writer Menander (342-292 B.C.). He is described bony faced and with sunken cheeks and eyes, and looking straight ahead. It is a late Roman copy of the original. The bust next to this one belongs to the famous philosopher Socrates. He is described wearing long hair, beard and moustache. His forehead is wide and he looks old. It was discovered with nose missing. Later, based on Socrates' description, a nose similar to that of Satyr Silenos was made.

Along the narrow wall in the direction of the exit, a section of one of the houses in Ephesus is recreated. In the arched niche in the middle of the wall is the statue of Artemis described as a hunter. It is a 4th century copy of the 1st century original. She is described as a young lady. In the predominantly red frescoe next to it, philosopher Socrates is depicted. Above his head is his name written in Greek. A similar frescoe has been discovered on a wall in one of the houses on the slopes. These are some of the unique pictures of the famous philosopher. The Socrates Frescoe was made in the 1st century A.D..

124 - Head of Eros, marble.

On the same wall are the other frescoes discovered together with the Socrates Frescoe. In one of them, a servant carrying a glass of drink; Demeter, the fertility goddess, sitting on her throne; and Eros, playing with his panther are shown. In the pool in front of this wall, household items such as an amphora, a millstone, an amphora with holes so that it could be kept in the sea to keep the fish put in it alive are on display. The mill in the pool was used to grind either wheat, to make flour, or salt. It is one of the items discovered in abundance in the houses.

The legs of the tables discovered in the houses on the slopes in Ephesus are taller than the ones used today and they are decorated with figures. In the main rooms of the houses, guests used to eat meals not sitting but reclining on benches. Since it was impossible to see the table top in this position, legs of the tables were usually shaped like statues. A table leg shaped like a statue of Dionysus, on display by the wall, is a good example. Dionysus is depicted either feeding or giving wine to his panther from a bowl.

THE HALL OF THE FOUNTAIN RELICS

During antiquity, fountains had an important place in urban architecture. They were built in significant locations in the city by affluent people. They were decorated with statues and columns, and all of them had one or two pools in the front. Those built during the Hellenistic age were small but appealing, and the ones built during the Empire were double-tiered and looked monumental.

A small door connects the Hall of the Residential Relics to the Hall of the Fountain Relics. The first object to the right of the entrance of this Hall

125 - Head of Zeus, marble. 1st century A.D..

is the Bust of Zeus. Although it exhibits the characteristics of the Classical era, it was created during the Roman Empire (1st century). The bust consists of two pieces. The smaller one was discovered later and put in place. Next to this is the marble statue of Aphrodite sculptured in ideal measurements. She is depicted naked above the hips, and both the head and the feet of the statue are missing. Both of these statues were created in the 1st century.

The tall statue in the centre is called the Resting Warrior and it was located in the triangular frontal of a fountain. He is depicted holding a sword in his left hand and reclining toward his shield.

The Polyphemus Group is in the round niche on the left side of the hall. This group was originally located on the pediment of the Temple of

126. The Resting Warrior, 1st century.

127 - The Polyphemus Group, 1st century B.C..

Augustus, but later it was placed on the edge of the pool of the Fountain of Pollio. Poseidon's son, Polyphemus, is depicted in tne middle. There are corpses in front of the person he killed on his knees. On one side of Polyphemus, Odysseus and his friends are depicted bringing him wine and on his other side, there are men carrying the pole prepared to blind Polyphemus. This group, too was created in the 1st century.

Opposite the Polyphemus Group are the statues from the Fountain of Trajan. The first statue depicts young Dionysus with his head leaning against a log. In front of him there are columns of vine, and beside him, a satyr is depicted lying down. Next to the wall are the statues of Dionysus and the members of the imperial family placed side by side. They are depicted dressed.

The diagram on the wall shows the original places of these statues on the Fountain of Trajan. The statues of Androklos the founder of Ephesus, with his dog, and Aphrodite are in front of diagram. Aphrodite is depicted semi-nude and with a sea shell covering her navel.

On the other side of the Hall are the statues from the Fountain of Laecanius Bassus, which is called the Aqua Palace. The one on the right, with feet like a sea serpent's, is the statue of Triton, Poseidon's son. The

128- Aphrodite, marble. 1st century.

129- Statues from the Laecanius Bassus Fountain, marble.

130- Head of a commander, marble. 1st century B.C.

*131 - Dionysus,
marble.
1st century A.D..*

*132 - Androklos.
marble.
1st century.*

*133 - Triton, marble.
1st century.*

*134 Nymph, marble.
1st century.*

other two statues depict the Nymphs. The outline of their bodies shows under the garments they are wearing.

One of the busts on the wall is the Bust of a Warrior. He is shown bearded and wearing a helmet, and it was made during the Roman Empire. It is a copy of the 5th century B.C. original. The other items are portraits and busts.

THE HALL OF THE RECENT FINDS

The main entrance of the Hall is through the Hall of the Fountain Relics. Small objects dating to the Byzantine era are displayed in the built in showcase to the right of this entrance. The bronze cross, and the other relics shaped like the cross, hanging on the white wall of the showcase, were made between the 6th and 12th centuries. Saint and the crucifix are depicted on some of them. The off-white glazed bowls decorated in the centre with birds are displayed on the floor of the showcase. They were made between the 10th and 12th centuries and decorated using the sgraffito technique. The fragment of an icon made of soapstone is ornamented with reliefs and exhibits high quality craftsmanship. The figures on it are bishops. This type of icon made of soapstone made its appearance in the 10th century. On one of the two small square panels displayed in this showcase, the Virgin Mary is depicted with Christ, and on the other panel, the Virgin Mary is depicted alone. These two silver panels with reliefs were parts of a box, and they are appliquéd onto the wall. The dark green coloured stone medallion is one of the most beautiful objects displayed in the showcase. On one side of the medallion Michael is depicted with wings, holding the Cross in one hand and a book in the other. On the other side of the medallion there is a man's head in the centre and seven animals with ears that are stretching their long bodies left and right. There is an inscription on each side of the medallion.

The coins are kept in the next few showcases. A diagram on the wall describes the way a coin was made in Ephesus. Two coins of Ephesus, one bearing the figure of a bee which is the symbol of Ephesus, and the other bearing a figure of Artemis, were enlarged and put on display here. Around the figure of Artemis is the inscription "Diana Ephesia", and on the other coin are the first two letters of the word "Ephesus" in Greek. Only a certain number of the coins unearthed during the excavations are being displayed.

135 - The Crosses, bronze. 5th-8th centuries.

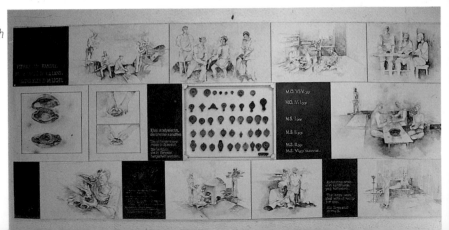

136- Oil lamps, 5th century, B.C.-11th century A.D..

137 - Tragedy Masks, marble. 2nd century.

In the small niche that comes after the one with coins there is a relics box containing the remais of a saint. It is shaped like a small sarcophagus. It was discovered in the Customs Building at the western end of the Harbour of Ephesus, and it dates back to the 8th century A.D...

A baptismal font is displayed in the third niche. It is shaped like a rosette with four leaves. Since its exterior is plain, it was used sunk in the ground. There is a votive inscription is Greek near its edge.

The head of the Bronze Serpent displayed in the second niche is missing. The snake depicted in motion was made to "protect" a house in the 1st century. It is covered with scales, and when examined closely, traces of gold plating can be seen.

In the fourth showcase, there are two statues of Eros. In one, a nude Eros is depicted standing and holding a mask in his left hand. With his right hand, which is missing, he was holding the lizard seen at his feet, by its tail. This statue was made to serve as the faucet of a fountain, and the water ran through the mouth of the mask. The other statue in the showcase depicts Eros on a dolphin and it was also made as a faucet. This type of fountain decorations popular even today, was used extensively in the Houses on the Slope in Ephesus.

Moulds are displayed in the last niche. The way the decorations were appliquéd on a Skyphos (wine bowl) is explained in the upper section of the showcase. This type of appliquéd ornamentation was first used in Pergamum during the Hellenistic period, and later it was used in the other cities also. The discovery of a positive mould in Ephesus indicates that the same method was used here, too. Oil lamps and other negative moulds, together with their prints, are displayed in the lower section of the showcase. Moulds made of baked clay and soapstone are seen on the right and these were used to cast weights.

The masks symbolizing tragedy are displayed to the left of the entrance

*138 - Frieze describing
the East campaign of
Emperor Traian, ivory,
1st century A.D.*

of the Hall of the Recent Finds. These masks were discovered during the excavations carried out at the Theatre of Ephesus. The sketches on the masks
indicate where they were used in theatres as decorations. Also, to emphasize
the fact that the actors used masks during performances, in the sketches,
the actors are depicted holding masks.

The oil lamp collection is the richest collection in the Ephesus Museum.
Most of the lamps discovered in the course of excavations were unearthed
in the Cave of the Seven Sleepers. We know that during antiquity, different
types of high quality oil lamps were produced in Ephesus and exported.
As in many other places, in the workshops in Ephesus, oil lamps were mass
produced using moulds. The way an oil lamp was made in Ephesus is
described in the sketches on the northern wall of the hall where oil lamps are
displayed. In the slim built-in showcase in the middle, examples of the oil
lamps discovered in Ephesus arc displayed, and the development of oil
lamps is described.

The bust of Emperor Marcus Aurelius is seen in the niche in the eastern
wall of the hall. It was discovered in an excellent state of preservation in
one of the Houses on the Slope. The Emperor's hair and beard are depicted
in large curls, and he is wearing a paludamentum fastened by a fibula on
the shoulder. The pose of Marcus Aurelius is not different from his other
statues other museums.

The Ivory Frieze, a rare treasure, is seen across the exit of the hall. It
was found in 1969 in one of the Houses on the Slope. The battle between
Emperor Trajan and the barbarians and the pre-war period are depicted
on the frieze. The main segment of the frieze consists of three panels. The
first caryatid on each side is depicted thinking, with one hand at her chin
and the other hand at her waist. The other caryatid is in such a bad shape
that it is impossible to tell her pose. The two Nikes between the panels

are looking at Emperor Trajan. On the first panel, Trajan is depicted wearing a short robe, and with a shield at his feet and a horse in front of him. On the other side of the horse there is a bearded figure wearing a long robe. He is presumed to be an important personality. Behind Trajan, there are Roman soldiers wearing war uniforms and carrying weapons. Behind the other figure, there are long haired and bearded soldiers. In the middle panel, Emperor Trajan is depicted in high relief in the front. In front of him, there is a warrior wearing an armour and a helmet, and he is about to give the horse to the Emperor. Rows of Roman soldiers are seen in the background. In the third panel, there are three, presumably eastern, warriors, a horse in motion, and in the background, rows of warriors. Besides these main panels, there are panels with scenes that complete the pre-war and post-war themes. The panel on the right describes a war scene and prisoners of war with their hands tied behind their backs.

The frieze was created during the reign of Emperor Trajan. Depth is achieved by placing the figures in the foreground in high relief and those in the background in low relief.

139 - Head of Emperor Marcus Aurelius, marble, 3rd century.

140 - Ivory. Frieze. 1st century

THE COURTYARD

Following the Hall of the Recent Finds comes the Middle Courtyard of the museum. Above the southern gallery of the courtyard the pediment of the Temple of Augustus (or of Isis) in the Ephesus State Agora is displayed. The pediment has been redone according to its original measurements. When the temple of Isis was destroyed either during an earthquake or due to another reason, the Ephesians moved the statues of the pediment to the Domitian Square and placed them around the pool of the Fountain of Pollio, thus changing the appearance of the fountain. They also converted the temple into a temple for Augustus in order to please the emperor. It is known that Emperor Augustus did not nurse warm feelings either for the Egyptians or for Egyptian religions because of Cleopatra and Antonius. The arrangement of the statues on the pediment in the courtyard is faithful to the original. In the middle is the gigantic Polyphemus, the son of Poseidon. He is described sitting. On his right, Odysseus is seen offering him wine from a bowl. Behind Odysseus there are men carrying wine in goat skin bags. The friends of Odysseus are seen at the other end of the pediment. They are sharpening the tip of a beam with their swords to get ready to poke out the eye of Odysseus after he gets drunk. The event is described in detail in the famous book "Odyssey" by Homer.

In the gallery under the pediment are examples of the columns discovered in Ephesus. These are displayed in chronological order. The Ionic capitals seen in the front row are the oldest examples of their kind in Ephesus. These were discovered during the restoration of St. Jean Aquaducts, and they date back to the 7th and 6th centuries B.C.. The Ionic capital decorated with a bull head was brought here from the Ephesus Basilica where it was used in the 1st century A.D.. The Corinthian and com-

posite capitals belong to Hellenistic and Roman structures. Those with stalactites were used in the Early Ottoman structures.

The steles appliqued onto the western wall of the courtyard belong to the Hellenistic era. When the steles are grouped according to style and theme, it becomes evident that in the Hellenistic era four workshops produced steles. Apparently, the earliest workshop started production in the 3rd century B.C.. Stele production gained momentum in the 2nd century. Since the artisans never signed their names on the steles, the names of the workshops are not known. On the stele, the deceased was described lying down, sitting or on a horse. On some of the steles mourning relatives are also depicted around the deceased. Some of the mourners are described with one hand raised, bidding farewell to the deceased.

Many sundials similar to the one displayed in the middle of the courtyard have been discovered in Ephesus. The concave dial is divided into

141 · Pediment of the Temple of Augustus, 1st century B.C..

142 · The Sundial, marble. 3rd century A.D.

twelve sections and each section is indicated by a different letter. The shadow of the thin rod in the exact center indicates time. From the inscription on its base we understand that the sundial was dedicated to Emperor Caracalla and his mother, Julia Domna (212-217 B.C.). The circles with sections seen on the sidewalks in Ephesus are sundials. It is possible to tell time by placing a stick in the center of these and observing its shadow.

An "Eros on a Dolphin" statue serves as the faucet of the fountain in the middle of the courtyard. These statues served similar functions in the Roman era.

The floor mosaic seen following the column capitals belongs to the living room of a building near the Vedius Gymnasium. The mosaic, decorated with geometric and plant motifs, date back to the 4th century A.D..

Following the mosaic one enters the Rear Courtyard. The most significant treasure displayed here is the inscription of 152 lines. Because of its importance, it is known as the Ephesus Monument. The inscription is about the Customs Regulations decleared by Emperor Nero on July 9th, 62. The rights of the Asian tax collectors and the rules they had to obey are described in detail in the inscription. In the Roman times, customs and taxes were not collected by civil servants like they are today but by private agencies who paid cash in advance to do this special job. As in many other provinces, in the Asian province, too, customs charge was 2.5% of the value of the goods. The text of the inscription describes the customs procedures. Travellers were required to show their belongings to the customs officials. For example, 5% luxury tax was charged for a purple dress. Food and anything else produced for the army, the Roman state and the emperor

143 - A grave stele, marble, 2nd century B.C.

were exempt from customs. Personal belongings, vehicles used during the trip and the slaves used as servants were also exempt from customs. However, the slaves that were considered trading goods were not exempt, and they were subject to tax known as the "head tax". The inscription, which had been erected in the harbour of Ephesus at a place easily seen by everybody, was relocated to the Church of St. John during the Byzantine era and used as an achitectural fragment in the ambo of the church.

The column with a Corinthian capital, the sarcophagus next to it and

144 - Inscription describing the Harbour Regulations, 2nd century A.D.

the griffins in the courtyard were brought from the Belevi Mausoleum located 13 kms to the north of Ephesus. The Belevi Mausoleum is similar to the mausoleum in Bodrum (Halicarnassus), which is considered one of the seven wonders of the world, but it is smaller. The Belevi Mausoleum, one of the largest Hellenistic mausoleums in Anatolia, is famous for being one of the first structures where Corinthian capitals were used. The mausoleum had a cubical burial chamber, and its main section was decorated with statues and columns. It was covered by a pyramidal roof with steps, and the sarcophagus was in the burial chamber. On the lid of the sarcophagus the deceased is described reclining. In the long and narrow frieze on the trunk of the sarcophagus there are eleven siren figures. In mythology, sirens were creatures with the body of a human and the head of a bird, and they led the deceased to Hades. The identity of the owner of the sarcophagus is not known definitely but it is assumed that it belonged to Antiochus II, the King of Seleucia who died in 246 B.C. near Ephesus. The marble griffin and the decorated sphere seen next to the sarcophagus belonged to the eaves of the pyramidal roof of the mausoleum. Other fragments of the eaves are next to the mausoleum in Belevi and some of them are in the Archaeological Museum in İzmir.

One of the other treasures in the Rear Courtyard worth mentioning is the sarcophagus with Muses. On the front and side surfaces of the sarcophagus there are niches with columns and arches, and in these niches Muses, who, in mythology, presided over literature and the arts and sciences, are depicted in low relief. Starting from left is Euterpe, carrying double flutes, and then, Clio, the muse of history. The face of the figure in the middle is quite distinct and the figure represents the owner of the sarcophagus, a lady. On the right are Calliope and Erato carrying a lute and a lyre. On the side surfaces are Melpomene and Thalia, the muses of comedy and tragedy. They are carrying theatre masks. On the other side is Urania carrying a sphere. She presided over astronomy. The one carrying a scepter is either Terpsichore, the muse of dance music, or Polyhymaia, the muse of pantomime. The sarcophagus was discovered near the Vedius Gymnasium in Ephesus and it dates back to the 3rd century A.D.. The sign of the cross and the inscription on its lid belong to the Byzantine era when it was reused.

The vaulted structure in the middle of the Rear Courtyard was used as an office building during the Seljouk era. It is assumed that originally the building was longer and that a section of it was torn down during the construction of the baths at a later date. At its entrance there used to be a dome supported by two columns but the dome has collapsed. The office buildings is positioned in accordance to the street with side-walks, passing in front of it. The street had been used until the late Ottoman period. Today, the building is used as the Conference Hall of the museum.

Next to the Conference Hall, samples of the millstones discovered in Ephesus and Selçuk are displayed. Mills, one of the most important ethnographic elements in Anatolia since the Neolithic times, were used to grind cereal, olives, salt, etc.. Hard stones, particularly bazalt, were used to make millstones. The earliest millstones discovered date back to the Calcholitic and Early Bronze Ages. These consist of two rectangular stones 30-40 cm. wide. The grain placed between the stones was ground manually by rubbing the two stones together. This type of millstones were discovered by chance in the region of Ephesus, only in the settlements in the Catstros

145- Sarcophagus with Muses, marble, 3rd century A.D.

valley. Those made of two circular millstones were more popular in home use. A handle used to be hooked onto the upper stone and turned manually to grind grain. This type of grinders were first used in the Hellenistic times and continued to be employed up to the late Ottoman period without being modified at all. Before the invention of hydromills, mills which were operated by one or two people by the help of a long pole had facilitated the task of grinding.

THE BATHS

The large, domed structure in the Rear Courtyard of the museum is one of the six baths built in the township of Selçuk during the Period of Principalities, and it is called the Saadet Hatun Baths. It was restored in 1979. In the Roman times, baths were an important part of everyday living, but they were almost completely forgotten in the West. However, the Seljouk and Ottoman Turks expanded and continued this tradition. The Saadet Hatun Baths is quite similar to the Roman baths and consists of a frigidarium (cold room), a tepidarium (warm room) and a caldarium (hot room). Although there is not a pool in the caldarium, there is a central massage slab known as "göbek taşı". Bathers come here first to lie down to rest and sweat in order to relax their muscles. According to Turkish customs, bath attendants known as "tellaks" give the bathers a special massage and rub them down with a special mitten made of coarse cloth. Also, according to a Muslim tradition, musical entertainments in baths were a part of wedding ceremonies. Today, Ottoman bath utensils are displayed in the Saadet Hatun Baths. These include pattens, towels, large bath towels and bowls which were used both by men and women. Traditionally, two baths, one for women and one for men, used to be built side by side and both were heated from a common boiler. Since the Saadet Hatun Bath is a single unit, there must have been special hours during the day for men and women.

THE HALL OF THE FUNERARY RELICS

The cemetery in Ephesus has not been excavated yet. The objects found in the graves discovered by chance in the course of excavations are exhibited in this hall.

Until the Byzantine era, it was traditional to place gifts in the graves, but during Christianity this tradition started to wane. The social status of the deceased, his financial situation and rank, dictated the size of the tomb built for him and the value of the gifts placed in these tombs.

On the right side of the hall, there is a sketch describing traditional burial ceremonies in Anatolia. Popular types of graves from the Old Bronze Age up to the Seljuk era are shown in the sketch. The oldest grave unearthed in Ephesus is a Mycenaen grave found by chance in the grounds of the Church of St. John. Gifts discovered in the grave were dated between 1400 and 1300 B.C. They are on display in the first showcase in the hall.

They were discovered during exploratory diggings carried on at the Agora (market place) of Ephesus. A Klazomenai-type sarcophagus dated to the 5th century B.C. is displayed with the gifts in it, in the centre of the hall. Some of the objects discovered in this type of sarcophagi are displayed in the second showcase.

146 - Stele of the grave of Olympia, daughter of Diocles, marble, 2nd century B.C..

The Cave of the Seven Sleepers was like a very popular cemetery during the early Christian era. Many graves, on top of each other, were found here where resurrection took place. Some of the objects discovered in this cave are displayed, along with the story of the seven sleepers, on the eastern wall of the hall. The picture seen on the right, is an enlarged copy of a 16th century miniature presently on display in the Museum of Turkish and Islamic Art in Istanbul. The miniature depicts the Muslim version of the story of the Seven Sleepers and their dog, Kitmir. The other drawing made in the 10th century was taken from the Saint Calendar of Basileus II, found in the Vatican. Here, the seven Christians, dressed according to the fashion of the day, are depicted sleeping.

Multi-coloured glass treasures seen in the showcase where the glass objects are displayed, are known as the Phoenician glassware. Some of these were discovered in Ephesus in the graves belonging to the Archaic period, and the others belong to the late Hellenistic and Roman eras. The bracelets seen in the lower section of the showcase belong to the Byzantine era.

147 - A Grave Stele, marble, 2nd century B.C.

148 - A Mycenean Bowl, 14th-13th centuries B.C..

149 - Bowls (presents) found in graves, 2nd century B.C.

150 - Osteotechs, marble, 1-3 A.D.

The stele dated to the 2nd century B.C. is seen next to this showcase. It has a frontal and bears an inscription. The tall figure in the centre is bidding farewell to his relatives, on his way to the other world. The large grave stele next to this was made to look like the facade of a Doric structure and the bust of the deceased is seen in a niche on the stele. She is depicted dressed and wearing a precious diadem. In order to protect the diadem made of a precious metal, the niche is blocked off with a grill. The inscription indicates that the stele belonged to Olympia, daughter of Diocles.

In the corner with a niche, the evolution of the mother goddess in Anatolia is described. The Statue of Cybele seen in the niche, is typical of other statues of Cybele found in museums in Turkey. She is depicted sitting on her throne with her lions on both sides of her. The statue was made in the 6th century B.C.. The others are steles of Cybele and have frontals. Cybele, Attis and Zeus are depicted together on these steles.

The main centres of the mother goddess in Turkey are indicated on the map next to these. Some of the treasures displayed in the built-in showcase next to this, were found in the well, (probably a wishing well) in the south-western corner of the state agora of Ephesus. Most of these objects belong to the 1st century B.C..

151 - A Grave Stele, marble, 1st century B.C.

152 - Statue of Cybele, marble, 4th century B.C.

THE HALL OF ARTEMIS

The statues of Artemis, the objects found at the temple and the altar of Artemis are displayed in this hall. The two most famous statues of Artemis in the museum are displayed on opposite sides. The one in the west is 2.92 metres tall and it is known as the Great Artemis. The one in the east is known as the Beautiful Artemis. Both of them were discovered at the Prytaneion (the administrative building) in Ephesus, in an excellent state of preservation.

153 - Artemis Ephesia, marble, 2nd century A.D.

154 - The Great Artemis, marble, 1st century A.D..

The Great Artemis looks Asian. The lions on both sides of Cybele had been reduced in size and placed on her shoulders. Her legs seem fused and her arms are stretched forward as though she is distributing fertility. With the gravity of a true goddess, she is looking beyond. The crown she is wearing has three tiers. Three Ionic temples, each with four columns in the facade, are seen on the uppermost tier, and griffons and sphinxes carrying arches are seen on the lower tiers. On each side of the moon behind her there are five lions and bull griffons. Her eyes are big, and her facial features are full. She wears earrings and two rows of necklaces.

There are four rows of nodes in the lower section of her chest. At first, these were assumed to be her breasts, then eggs, and according to a recent theory, they represent the testes of the bulls sacrificed for the goddess. All these are based on the idea of fertility and reproduction. Although the goddess was a virgin, she was the protectress of women giving birth.

Her forearms are broken. The hole seen in her right arm could have been made either during a restorations, or to attach the arm made of a precious metal like gold.

During antiquity, the goddess used to be dressed in clothes made of very valuable fabrics and only her face and arms were exposed. Therefore, it is possible that her hands had been made of gold. She is wearing a narrow belt decorated with motifs of a rosette of four segments and a bee (symbol of Ephesus). The base of the statue is missing. Her skirt which hangs straight is separated into rectangles by horizontal and vertical lines. In each rectangle, there are figures of animals such as lions, bulls, deer, rams, griffons and bees. There are six rectangles in each row. On the sides of her skirt, there is only one figure in each rectangle. In the middle rectangle of the first five rows, there are three figures and in the middle rectangle of the sixth row there are two figures.

155- Lion's Head, ivory, 7th century B.C..

156- An Artemision Priestess, gold, 7th century B.C.

157- Megabysos, the Priest of the Temple of Artemis, ivory, 7th century B.C..

The Great Artemis was made in the 1st century A.D.

The Beautiful Artemis which stands 1.74 metres tall was made about 50 years after the Great Artemis and resembles it. It was made from better quality marble. It is whiter, well-glazed and was gold-gilded. Traces of the gilding can be seen only on the right side of her neck. Her crown is missing. Figures of Nike decorate the upper section of her necklace which resembles strands of pearls, and signs of the zodiac decorate the lower section of her necklace. Her skirt tapers towards her feet and only the tips of her toes are exposed. Her sacred animals, deer, are seen on both sides of her.

There is another small statue of Artemis next to the statue of Beautiful Artemis. The head of the statue is missing and on her chest are the figures of Nike and signs of the zodiac. Both statues were created about the same time.

158 - Part of a Statue of Artemis. 1st century B.C..

159 - An Artemision Priestess, ivory, 7th century B.C.

160 - A disc, ivory, 6th century B.C.

161 - Water pipe from the Artemision, lead, 1st century A.D.

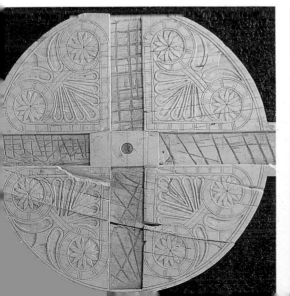

162 - Relics from the Artemision, gold and ivory, 7th century B.C..

163 - Necklace beads, gold, 6th century B.C.

The Torso of Artemis seen in the showcase was unearthed during the excavation of a street. Dated to the 1st century B.C., this statue of Artemis bears three figures of either bull or deer heads on her chest.

The Gold Statu, which is seen in the showcase, is dated to the 7th century B.C. and it belongs to a goddess. It was discovered during the excavation of the Artemision. There are many ivory statues which resemble this statue. The votive offerings which look like crystal wine goblets are actually made of rock crystal. There are very few of these in the museums of the world. The baked clay, marble, ivory, bronze and gold objects in the showcase were made between the 7th and the 5th centuries B.C. and were offered to the temple. The ivory statuette of a ram is Cimmerian.

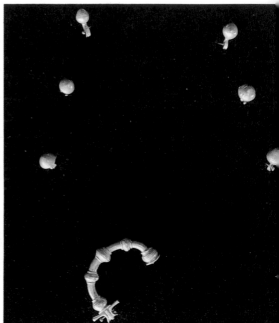

The relief of an Amazon seen in the hall is a copy.

The statue of a horse is one of the four horses on a statue of a quadriga (a chariot drawn by 4 horses) created in the 4th century B.C.. The quadriga was discovered on the altar of Artemis. The architectural elements of the temple are placed according to their original order.

The head of a young man seen in the hall is a part of one of the columnae caelatae (sculptured columns)

165 - Portraits. 2nd and 3rd centuries.

166 - Head of a Man, marble, 2nd century A.D..   *167- Head of a Woman, marble, 3rd century A.D..*

THE HALL OF THE IMPERIAL CULTS AND PORTRAITS

The Roman period was the golden age of Ephesus. The most important monuments in the city were built in this age. Ephesus was given the right to become a neokoros (the privilage of owning an imperial temple) four times and thus established superiority over the rival cities of Samos, Pergamum and Smyrna. Among the imperial temples, the locations of the temples of Dominian and Olympeion are known but those of the temples of Caracalla and Valerianus are not. The excavation of the temple of Domitian has been completed, its altar along with the colossal head of the emperor's statue and other artifacts have been brought to the museum. In 128, when Emperor Hadrian returned to Ephesus from Athens as Zeus Olympios, he gave permission to build an imperial temple and the Ephesians built the temple of Olympeion, the fourth largest temple in Anatolia. Since the temple was used as a stone and lime quarry during the Byzantine era and most of its parts were used in the construction of the city walls, the temple is in ruins. The excavation of the Olympeion has not been completed yet.

The statue seen on the left upon entrance into the hall belongs to Consul Stefanos. He is described holding his scepter in one hand and a handkerchief in the other which is raised as though he is about to signal the start of a game or a race. The statue, made in the 6th century A.D., is typical of the Byzantian portraits. The first of the six portraits displayed on the wall was created in the 3rd century. The others were also made in the same period and they belong to the distinguished citizens of Ephesus.

On the western wall of the hall is the picture of the small temple of Hadrian on the Curetes Street. The frieze of the temple is displayed on both sides of the picture. The frieze consists of four sections. In the first three sections on the left certain gods and goddesses. Androclos, the legendary founder of Ephesus, chasing the boar on horseback; gods and the Amazons who occupy an important place in Ephesian mythology; and the Amazons and a Dionysiac procession are described. The theme depicted in the fourth section is different. Starting from left, Athena; Selena; an

168 - Bust of a woman, marble, 1st century A.D.

169 - Portrait of Emperor Traian, marble, 98-117 A.D.

170 - Bust of a man, marble, 3rd century A.D.

171 - Portrait of Emperor Germanicus, marble, 15 B.C., 19 A.D.

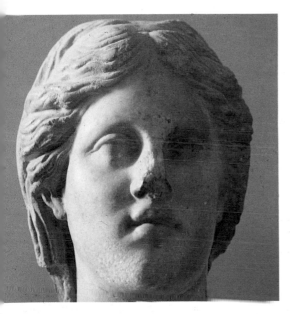

172 - Statue of Consul Stephanos, marble, 6th century A.D.

unknown man; Appolon; an unknown woman; Androclos; Heracles, the father of Emperor Theodosius; Theodosius; Artemis; the wife and the son of Theodosius and Athena are described in a row. The first three sections of the frieze date back to the reign of Emperor Hadrian (2nd century A.D.) but this last section must have been redone and placed here during the restorations in the 4th century.

173 - Frieze of the Temple of Hadrian, 2nd century A.D..

Two of the three statue heads seen after the frieze of the temple of Hadrian are the Ideal Women heads (Artemis?) and the other is the portrait of a man, and it demonstrates a distinct style. The head of Emperor Traian, seen in the same row, is one of the most beautiful and valuable